Everyman's Poetry

Everyman, I will go with thee,
and be thy guide

Robert Louis Stevenson

Selected and edited by JENNI CALDER

EVERYMAN

J. M. Dent · London

This edition first published by Everyman Paperbacks in 1997

Selection, introduction and other critical apparatus
© J. M. Dent 1997

J. M. Dent
Orion Publishing Group
Orion House
5 Upper St Martin's Lane,
London WC2H 9EA

Typeset by Deltatype Ltd, Birkenhead, Merseyside
Printed in Great Britain by
The Guernsey Press Co. Ltd., Guernsey, C. I.

British Library Cataloguing-in-Publication Data
is available upon request.

ISBN 0 460 87809 3

Contents

from *A Child's Garden of Verses (1885)*

from *Ballads (1890)*

from *Songs of Travel (1895)*

Poems first published in fiction and later poems published posthumously

Note on the Author and Editor

ROBERT LOUIS STEVENSON was born in Edinburgh in 1850. An only child of professional middle-class parents he was often ill and had no regular schooling. In 1867 he began to study engineering, his father's profession, at Edinburgh University but secretly wanted to be a writer. He spent much of his time leading a bohemian life and exploring the underside of Edinburgh. In 1871 his father accepted his intention to become a writer on condition that he studied for the Bar, but Stevenson had no plans to practise as a lawyer. He began visiting an artists' colony in France, where he met Fanny Osbourne, whom he married in 1880.

While still a student Stevenson committed himself to a rigorous apprenticeship as a writer, and began to publish seriously in 1873. He initially published in magazines, with his first book, *An Inland Voyage*, appearing in 1878. Although recognised by a few as a writer of promise, it took some years for him to establish a reputation, beginning with *Treasure Island* in 1883, receiving critical acclaim for *Kidnapped* in 1886 and reaching bestseller status with *Strange Case of Dr Jekyll and Mr Hyde* in the same year. His first volume of poetry was *A Child's Garden of Verses* in 1885.

His precarious state of health made it impossible for him to live permanently in Scotland, and in 1887, after the death of his father, he went to the United States, where his reputation preceded him. Now a successful writer, with the added support of his father's legacy, he set off to fulfil a dream of voyaging in the South Pacific. He, Fanny and other members of their family left San Francisco in June 1888 and spent the next two years exploring the South Seas. Stevenson's health was much improved, and in 1890 he settled in Samoa where he bought land and built a house. He never returned to Scotland. All this time he was writing poetry, fiction, and accounts of his South Sea experiences, and being published enthusiastically in Britain and the United States. He died suddenly of a brain haemorrhage on 3 December 1894, leaving several unfinished works, including *Weir of Hermiston*, considered by many to be his best piece of fiction. He wrote poetry throughout his career and published three volumes in his lifetime.

JENNI CALDER is author and editor of several books on Stevenson, including *RLS: A Life Study* (Hamish Hamilton, 1980 and Richard Drew, 1990), and has edited a number of his works. She is Head of Publishing at the National Museums of Scotland and Edinburgh. Her most recent book is *The Nine Lives of Naomi Mitchison* (Virago, 1997). She publishes poetry as Jenni Daiches.

Chronology of Stevenson's Life

Year	Age	Life
1850		Born 13 November in Edinburgh, only child of Margaret Isabella Balfour and Thomas Stevenson, lighthouse and harbour engineer
1857	7	The family begins living at 17 Heriot Row in Edinburgh's New Town. Stevenson's schooling sporadic as he was often ill

Chronology of his Times

Year	Literary Context	Historical Events
1850	Tennyson becomes Poet Laureate; Death of Honoré de Balzac	First Public Libraries Act passed
1852	Thackeray, *Henry Esmond* Hawthorne, *Tanglewood Tales*	The Earl of Derby becomes prime minister Napoleon III becomes emperor of France
1853	Dickens, *Bleak House* Verdi produces *La Traviata* and *Il Trovatore*	
1857	Baudelaire, *Les Fleurs du Mal* Trollope, *Barchester Towers*	Indian Mutiny breaks out
1858	George Macdonald, *Phantastes* Dean Ramsay, *Reminiscences of Scottish Life* Ballantyne, *Coral Island*	
1861		Death of Prince Albert, husband of Queen Victoria Victor Emmanuel II becomes first king of a united Italy American Civil War breaks out
1863	Tolstoy begins publication of *War and Peace* Margaret Oliphant, *Salem Chapel*	

Year	Age	Life
1867	17	Begins to study engineering at University of Edinburgh
1871	21	Announces his attention to become a writer, and switches his studies to law
1873	23	Meets his long-term friend and mentor, Sidney Colvin, and first serious love Mrs Fanny Sitwell. Spends winter in South of France for his health. Publishes his first article
1875	25	Meets W. E. Henley, friend and collaborator. First of many visits to Fontainebleau area of France. Called to the Scottish bar
1876	26	Meets Fanny Osbourne
1878	28	*An Inland Voyage*, his first book, published

Year	Literary Context	Historical Events
1866	Dostoevsky, *Crime and Punishment* John Henry Newman, *The Dream of Gerontius*	Atlantic telegraph cable is laid
1867	Arnold, *Culture and Anarchy*	Second Reform Act passed
1869		Imprisonment for debt abolished Bedford College for women incorporated in University of London First railway across America completed
1871	George Eliot, *Middlemarch*	Bank holidays introduced William I becomes first German emperor Henry Morton Stanley meets Dr Livingstone at Ujiji
1872	Samuel Butler, *Erewhon*	First University College opens at Aberystwyth
1873	Rimbaud, *Une Saison d'Enfer*	Ashanti War breaks out Death of Dr Livingstone
1874	Strauss, *Die Fledermaus* James Thomson, *The City of Dreadful Night*	Benjamin Disraeli becomes prime minister
1875	Death of Hans Christian Andersen	Disraeli purchases Suez Canal shares on Britain's behalf
1876	Twain, *The Adventures of Tom Sawyer*	Queen Victoria becomes Empress of India Bulgarian Christians massacred by Turkish irregular troops
1877		Russo-Turkish war breaks out in Balkans
1878	Tchaikovsky, *Eugene Onegin*	Zulu War begins Congress of Berlin meets to solve Balkans crisis

Year	Age	Life
1879	29	Follows Fanny Osbourne to California. *Travels With a Donkey* published. Begins to be recognised as a writer of talent
1880	30	Marries Fanny Osbourne. Honeymoon at Silverado, a deserted Californian mining camp. Returns to Scotland with Fanny and stepson Lloyd. *Deacon Brodie*, a drama collaboration with W. E. Henley, published. Goes to Davos, Switzerland, for his health, summers in Scotland
1881	31	Writes *Treasure Island*. *Virginibus Puerisque* (essays) published
1882	32	Moves to South of France for his health, summers in Scotland. Works on *A Child's Garden of Verses*. *Familiar Studies of Men and Books* (essays) and *New Arabian Nights* published
1883	33	*Treasure Island* published; reputation as fiction writer established. *The Silverado Squatters* published
1884	34	Moves to Bournemouth. Forms close friendship with Henry James
1885	35	*A Child's Garden of Verses* and *Prince Otto* published. Writes *Kidnapped* and *Strange Case of Dr Jekyll and Mr Hyde*
1886	36	*Strange Case of Dr Jekyll and Mr Hyde* published; becomes a bestseller. *Kidnapped* published to critical acclaim

Year	Literary Context	Historical Events
1879	Ibsen produces *A Doll's House* James, *Daisy Miller*	
1880	George Newnes starts *Tit-Bits* de Maupassant publishes his first stories in *Boule de Suif*	William Ewart Gladstone becomes prime minister
1881	Death of Thomas Carlyle	Death of Disraeli First Boer War breaks out Alexander III becomes Tsar of Russia
1882	Publication begins of *Dictionary of National Biography*	Married Woman's Property Act passed Pretoria Convention ends Boer War Triple Alliance formed between Italy, Austria and Germany
1883	Birth of Compton Mackenzie Death of Edward Fitzgerald, author of *The Rubaiyat of Omar Khayyam*	
1884	Publication begins of the *Oxford English Dictionary*	Fabian Society founded Third Reform Act passed
1885		Earl of Salisbury becomes prime minister Death of General Charles Gordon at Khartoum Death of General Ulysses S. Grant
1886	Hardy, *The Mayor of Casterbridge* Death of Emily Dickinson	First Irish Home Rule Bill fails

Year	Age	Life
1887	37	Death of his father, Thomas Stevenson. Travels to USA with Fanny and Mrs Stevenson. Winter at Saranac in the Adirondack Mountains. *Underwoods* and *Memories and Portraits* (essays) published. Begins writing *The Master of Ballantrae*
1888	38	To San Francisco. Hires yacht *Casco* and begins first South Pacific voyages. Health very much improved. Begins the writing of articles and fiction based on South Seas experiences. *The Master of Ballantrae* and *The Black Arrow* published
1889	39	Six months in Hawaii, second Pacific voyage on the *Equator*. First visit to Samoa. *The Wrong Box*, written with Lloyd Osbourne, published
1890	40	Buys Vailima on the island of Upolu, Samoa. Third Pacific voyage on the *Janet Nichol* after illness in Sydney, Australia. Realises that a return to Europe is unlikely and settles at Vailima. *Ballads* published
1890 –94		At Vailima with Fanny and extended family. Writes *The Beach of Falesa*, *The Ebb-Tide*, as well as fiction and poetry inspired by memories of Scotland. *In the South Seas* published
1892	42	*The Wrecker* (with Lloyd Osbourne) and *A Footnote to History* published
1893	43	*Catriona* published

Year	Literary Context	Historical Events
1887	Birth of Edwin Muir Arthur Conan Doyle publishes the first Sherlock Holmes story, *A Study in Scarlet*	Queen Victoria's Golden Jubilee
1888	August Strindberg produces *Miss Julie*	Jack the Ripper murders six women in London John Boyd Dunlop produces pneumatic tyres William II becomes German emperor
1889	Death of Gerard Manley Hopkins W. B. Yeats, *The Wanderings of Oisin* J. M. Barrie, *A Window in Thrums*	First London dock strike
1890		Bismarck is dismissed as chancellor Parnell/O'Shea divorce case Henri de Toulouse-Lautrec produces first Moulin Rouge paintings
1891	Birth of Neil Gunn	Elementary school fees abolished Paul Gauguin settles in Tahiti
1892	Oscar Wilde produces *Lady Windermere's Fan* Birth of Hugh MacDiarmid	
1893	Sir Arthur Wing Pinero produces *The Second Mrs Tanqueray*	Matabele rising Second Irish Home Rule Bill fails Civil war breaks out in Samoa

Year	Age	Life
1894	44	Dies suddenly on 3 December of a cerebral haemorrhage, leaving *Weir of Hermiston* and *St Ives* unfinished. *The Ebb-Tide* published

Year	Literary Context	Historical Events
1894	Kipling, *The Jungle Book* John Buchan publishes his first book, *Essays and Apothegms of Francis Lord Bacon* du Maurier, *Trilby* Gissing, *In the Year of Jubilee* George Moore, *Esther Waters* Hope, *The Prisoner of Zenda*	Death of Louis Kossuth Earl of Rosebery becomes prime minister

Introduction

Although Robert Louis Stevenson's reputation is primarily as a writer of fiction, among the books for which he is best remembered is *A Child's Garden of Verses*, published in 1885 when *Treasure Island* had already introduced him as a writer with considerable child appeal. These books have for generations influenced the response to Stevenson and masked his achievement as a writer for adults. This has especially affected the reading of his poetry.

By the time he was twenty Stevenson was sure that he wanted writing to be his profession. He was ready to try his hand at almost anything and experimented widely. This naturally included verse. He cheerfully imitated past and current forms and voices, translated from French, German and Latin, and wrote in Scots. This last was particularly important to him. He loved the language – he insisted that it was a language, and not a collection of dialects – and used it always with conviction, often with a playful exuberance. Although Stevenson's literary career was established first through essays and travel writing and then through fiction, he never stopped writing poetry and produced some of his most memorable poems towards the end of his life.

An authoritative collection of Stevenson's poetry did not appear until 1950, when Janet Adam Smith's edition was published. She emphasises the range and variety of his output, and its qualities as occasional verse. This has particular significance in the context of the subjects and tone of his prose writing, in which, at least before 1879, it was rare for him to write directly about the personal or the contemporary. His poetry shows him responding more candidly to emotional and social challenges which, for complex reasons of parentage and upbringing, it took him much longer to learn to handle in prose. So 'occasional' doesn't necessarily mean superficial, however ephemeral the occasions themselves may have been. Much of his early poetry is charged with immediacy and emotional intensity, especially when he moves away from formality of metre and language and writes free verse. Good examples are 'My brain swims empty and light . . .' and 'Song at Dawn'. His experiments with free verse and sturdier language owe much to his discovery of Walt Whitman in the early 1870s.

By the 1880s Stevenson had written a substantial body of poetry on which he drew to put together his collection *Underwoods* which was published in 1887. He himself didn't rate his poetry very highly – 'I have begun to learn some of the rudiments of [writing verse], and have written three or four pretty enough pieces of octosyllabic nonsense, semi-serious, semi-smiling,' he wrote to his friend W. E. Henley in April 1883. But *Underwoods* was generally well received by the critics, although there were those who flinched at what they considered to be indelicacy. The qualities which appealed to his contemporaries – an attractive freshness and sincerity, and easiness on the ear – survive well, even where ornate or archaic diction jars. But a hallmark of Stevenson's poetry at its best is a vivid immediacy. He can catch a moment, a mood, a movement in a way which can illuminate otherwise unexceptional verse. A good exampled is this image from 'To Mrs Will H. Low' which leaps invigoratingly off the page:

> . . . in the chequered silence and above
> The hum of city cabs that sought the Bois,
> Surburban ashes shivered into song.
> A patter and a chatter and a chirp
> And a long dying hiss – it was as though
> Starched old brocaded dames through all the house
> Had trailed a strident skirt . . .

When Stevenson combines this immediacy with authentic and resonant emotion his poetry becomes highly rewarding. Some of the poems he wrote towards the end of his life, in which he remembers Scotland from the other side of the world, achieve this:

> Blows the wind today, and the sun and the rain are flying,
> Blows the wind on the moors today and now,
> Where about the graves of the martyrs the whaups are crying,
> My heart remembers how.

The simplicity here is counterpointed by the inversion which introduces an interrogative note, and by the use of the present tense which implies a contradiction of the idea of memory. The poem, 'To S. R. Crockett', goes on to confirm a sense of loss, but in this opening stanza there is a rich ambivalence in the intensity and almost wistful uncertainty of remembered experience.

Stevenson published one other collection of poetry in his lifetime, *Ballads* of 1890, although he was preparing a fourth, *Songs of Travel*, at the time of his death in December 1894. He was attracted by the ballad form through his immersion in Scottish legend and traditional tales and this interest was reactivated when he encountered Polynesian legend during his South Pacific travels. He found that swapping stories and poems was an excellent means of establishing a rapport with the island peoples he encountered, and in particular formed a highly creative relationship with Prince Ori a Ori and Princess Moe of Tautira in Tahiti. This gave him the basis of his long narrative poem 'The Song of Rahéro', which he retells with a sympathetic understanding of its origins. A shorter ballad included here, 'Heather Ale', is quite different in tone and effect.

Most of Stevenson's frequently anthologised poems come from *Songs of Travel* (1896), which reflects the impact of his South Sea experiences. Like his first visit to the United States, in 1879 when he followed Fanny Osbourne, whom he eventually married, to California, his Pacific voyages affected both the content and the style of his writing. This is most robustly expressed in his prose, but his poetry reveals the contrary influences and pressures that were at work. He loved the Pacific islands and entered into life in Samoa, where he settled in 1890, with a fascinated commitment. At the same time, he longed for Scotland. That longing, as 'To S. R. Crockett' shows, was most directly expressed in poetry. But *Songs of Travel* also includes poems celebrating Pacific experiences in particular and the whole notion of travel in general. Perhaps the best known of the latter is 'The Vagabond' – 'Give to me the life I love,/ Let the lave go by me'.

> Wealth I ask not, hope nor love,
>   Let what will be o'er me;
> All I ask the heaven above,
>   And the road below me.

'The Vagabond' was written 'to an air of Schubert' (and has been set to music by more than one twentieth-century composer) and raises another aspect of Stevenson's poetry. Many of his poems, whether or not actually written to a specific tune – and quite a number were – have a song-like quality which is a significant feature of their appeal. His talent for lyrical simplicity invites a musical setting.

'Charming' is the word commonly used to describe Stevenson's poems about childhood. This, however, does not do justice to the layered and often complex nature of much of what is included in *A Child's Garden of Verses* and belies the dark and troubled mood of some of the poems. The collection captures contrasting aspects of childhood experience, from the imaginative play of 'Pirate Story', to the more reflective 'Travel' and 'Keepsake Mill' and the wistful longing of 'The Lamplighter', the irony of 'My Shadow', and the terror and loneliness of 'North-West Passage'. Certainly, Stevenson has an extraordinary talent for illuminating a child's view of the world, but it is, again, the emotional authenticity that makes these poems so valuable, and memorable reading for the adult as much as the child. The same can be said of those poems of Stevenson's which can sometimes tremble on the edge of sentimentality. There is nothing synthetic about:

> I will make you brooches and toys for your delight
> Of bird-song at morning and star-shine at night.

It has a luminous precision which defies the sentimental.

Whatever the tone or mood of Stevenson's poems, certain themes and preoccupations emerge which unify his output. One of these is travel, the sense of movement and above all of freedom, but this is inseparable from a preoccupation with what has been left behind, both places and people. Whatever the call of 'over the hills and far away' ('A Song of the Road'), the meaning of distance depends on the starting point. Writing in the South Pacific, 'the tropics vanish' and he is back in the Pentland Hills of his Edinburgh youth, or, in 'To S. C.', he is thinking of his friend and mentor, Sidney Colvin, back in London:

> So far, so foreign, your divided friends
> Wander, estranged in body, not in mind.

Physical distance intensifies certain kinds of experience, and reading Stevenson's expressions of loss – of his youth, of Scotland, perhaps more than anything of direct contact with his own history, 'the voice of generations dead' – suggests that in poetic terms his

voyaging was all about the intensification of remembered experience, emotion not so much recollected in tranquillity as sharpened
by distance.

The most important 'lost' person was probably Stevenson's
father, who profoundly influenced his life and work. Thomas
Stevenson was much loved and admired by his son, but also much
rebelled against. Although Stevenson decided to become a writer
rather than follow his father's profession of lighthouse engineer, his
tributes to his father recur, in 'To My Father' and in recurring
images of lighthouses, light-keepers and the protecting of ships and
seamen. A more painful aspect of rebellion was Stevenson's break
away from his Calvinist upbringing, which is reflected in some of
his early poems. But Stevenson wasn't able fully to escape his
father's hold until Thomas Stevenson's death in 1887, and even
then his father's shadow can be detected in much of his poetry's
fundamental tension: adventure and authority, savageness and
security, recklessness and responsibility. Throughout his life
Stevenson was conscious of these contradictory pulls and they fed
all of his writing.

Stevenson's poetic voice is erratic but this reflects his pleasure in
writing about greatly varied topics and experiences. It is also part of
the reader's pleasure. Not to be underestimated are his playful
verse-making, his sheer delight in words and stories, and his good-
humoured and often entertaining satire:

> They had at first a human air
> In coats and flannel underwear.
> They rose and walked upon their feet
> And filled their bellies full of meat.
> They wiped their lips when they had done,
> But they were Ogres every one.

But his most effective poetry illustrates the power of language and
imagination to create a lasting image out of loss, and in that he
could be flawless, as in 'To Any Reader':

> As from the house your mother sees
> You playing round the garden trees,
> So you may see, if you will look
> Through the windows of this book,
> Another child, far, far away,
> And in another garden, play.

> But do not think you can at all,
> By knocking on the window, call
> That child to you. He intent
> Is all on his play-business bent.
> He does not hear; he will not look,
> Nor yet be lured out of this book.
> For, long ago, the truth to say,
> He has grown up and gone away,
> And it is but a child of air
> That lingers in the garden there.

This is Stevenson at his best, simple but containing rich layers of meaning, a regular rhyme but rhythmically challenging, creating vivid imagery that holds complex ideas of time, experience and the imagination.

'To Any Reader' is an envoi attached to *A Child's Garden of Verses*. I feel it is a great disservice to Stevenson to separate his poems about childhood from the rest of his work, and although I have grouped his poetry according to the published volumes, I have placed the *Child's Garden* poems where I believe they fit in the roughly chronological sequence. A few of Stevenson's poems have been much anthologised, but his poetry as a whole has been largely overlooked with most of it long out of print. This selection has been chosen to show his range and versatility as well as to demonstrate the rewards of reading his poetry. It is the work of a writer of extraordinary sensitivity, equally at home with the serious and the ridiculous, equally responsive to simple beauties and complex anxieties.

JENNI CALDER

Robert Louis Stevenson

Early poems published posthumously

Duddingston

1

With caws and chirrupings, the woods
   In this thin sun rejoice,
The Psalm seems but the little kirk
   That sings with its own voice.

The cloud-rifts share their amber light   5
   With the surface of the mere –
I think the very stones are glad
   To feel each other near.

Once more my whole heart leaps and swells
   And gushes o'er with glee: 10
The fingers of the sun and shade
   Touch music stops in me.

2

Now fancy paints that bygone day
   When you were here, my fair –
The whole lake rang with rapid skates   15
   In the windless, winter air.

You leaned to me, I leaned to you,
   Our course was smooth as flight –
We steered – a heel-touch to the left,
   A heel-touch to the right.   20

We swung our way through flying men,
   Your hand lay fast in mine,

We saw the shifting crowd dispart,
  The level ice-reach shine.

I swear by yon swan-travelled lake,   25
  By yon calm hill above,
I swear had we been drowned that day
  We had been drowned in love.

The Light-Keeper

1

The brilliant kernel of the night,
The flaming lightroom circles me:
I sit within a blaze of light
Held high above the dusky sea.
Far off the surf doth break and roar   5
Along bleak miles of moonlit shore,
Where through the tides the tumbling wave
Falls in an avalanche of foam
And drives its churned waters home
Up many an undercliff and cave.   10

The clear bell chimes: the clockworks strain,
The turning lenses flash and pass,
Frame turning within glittering frame
With frosty gleam of moving glass:
Unseen by me, each dusky hour   15
The sea-waves welter up the tower
Or in the ebb subside again;
And ever and anon all night,
Drawn from afar by charm of light,
A sea bird beats against the pane.   20

And lastly when dawn ends the night
And belts the semi-orb of sea,
The tall, pale pharos in the light

Looks white and spectral as may be.
The early ebb is out: the green   25
Straight belt of seaweed now is seen,
That round the basement of the tower
Marks out the interspace of tide;
And watching men are heavy-eyed,
And sleepless lips are dry and sour.   30

The night is over like a dream:
The sea-birds cry and dip themselves:
And in the early sunlight, steam
The newly bared and dripping shelves,
Around whose verge the glassy wave   35
With lisping wash is heard to lave;
While, on the white tower lifted high,
The circling lenses flash and pass
With yellow light in faded glass
And sickly shine against the sky.   40

2

As the steady lenses circle
With a frosty gleam of glass;
And the clear bell chimes,
And the oil brims over the lip of the burner,
Quiet and still at his desk,   45
The lonely Light-Keeper
Holds his vigil.

Lured from far,
The bewildered seagull beats
Dully against the lantern;   50
Yet he stirs not, lifts not his head
From the desk where he reads,
Lifts not his eyes to see
The chill blind circle of night
Watching him through the panes.   55
This is his country's guardian,
The outmost sentry of peace.
This is the man

Who gives up that is lovely in living
For the means to live.   60

Poetry cunningly gilds
The life of the Light-Keeper,
Held on high in the blackness
In the burning kernel of night,
The seaman sees and blesses him,   65
The Poet, deep in a sonnet,
Numbers his inky fingers
Fitly to praise him.
Only we behold him,
Sitting, patient and stolid,   70
Martyr to a salary.

My brain swims empty and light . . .

My brain swims empty and light
Like a nut on a sea of oil;
And an atmosphere of quiet
Wraps me about from the turmoil and clamour of life.

I stand apart from living,   5
Apart and holy I stand,
In my new-gained growth of idleness, I stand,
As stood the Shekinah of yore in the holy of holies.

I walk the streets smoking my pipe
And I love the dallying shop-girl   10
That leans with rounded stern to look at the fashions;
And I hate the bustling citizen,
The eager and hurrying man of affairs I hate,
Because he bears his intolerance writ on his face
And every movement and word of him tells me how much he
   hates me.   15

I love night in the city,
The lighted streets and the swinging gait of harlots.
I love cool pale morning,
In the empty bye-streets,
With only here and there a female figure,   20
A slavey with lifted dress and the key in her hand,
A girl or two at play in a corner of waste-land
Tumbling and showing their legs and crying out to me loosely.

The Cruel Mistress

Here let me rest, here nurse the uneasy qualm
That yearns within me;
And to the heaped-up sea,
Sun-spangled in the quiet afternoon,
Sing my devotions.   5

In the sun, at the edge of the down,
The whin-pods crackle
In desultory volleys;
And the bank breathes in my face
Its hot sweet breath –   10
Breath tht stirs and kindles,
Lights that suggest, not satisfy –
Is there never in life or nature
An opiate for desire?
Has everything here a voice,   15
Saying '*I am not the goal;*
Nature is not to be looked at alone;
Her breath, like the breath of a mistress,
Her breath also,
Parches the spirit with longing   20
Sick and enervating longing.'

Well, let the matter rest.
I rise and brush the windle-straws
Off my clothes; and lighting another pipe

Stretch myself over the down.   25
Get thee behind me, Nature!
I turn my back on the sun
And face from the grey new town at the foot of the bay.

I know an amber lady
Who has her abode   30
    At the lips of the street
In prisons of coloured glass.
I had rather die of her love
Than sicken for you, O Nature!
Better be drunk and merry   35
Than dreaming awake!
Better be Falstaff than Obermann!

Storm

The narrow lanes are vacant and wet;
The rough wind bullies and blusters about the township.
And spins the vane on the tower
And chases the scurrying leaves,
And the straw in the damp innyard.   5
See – a girl passes
Tripping gingerly over the pools,
And under her lifted dress
I catch the gleam of a comely, stockinged leg.
Pah! the room stifles me,   10
Reeking of stale tobacco –
With the four black mealy horrible prints
After Landseer's pictures.
I will go out.

Here the free wind comes with a fuller circle,   15
Sings, like an angry wasp, in the straining grass,
Sings and whistles;
And the hurried flow of rain
Scourges my face and passes.

Behind me, clustered together, the rain-wet roofs of the town   20
Shine, and the light vane shines as it veers
In the long pale finger of sun that hurries across them to me.
The fresh salt air is keen in my nostrils,
And far down the shining sand
Foam and thunder   25
And take the shape of the bay in eager mirth
The white-head hungry billows.
The earth shakes
As the semicircle of waters
Stoops and casts itself down;   30
And far outside in the open,
Wandering gleams of sunshine
Show us the ordered horde that hurries to follow.

Ei! merry companions,
Your madness infects me.   35
My whole soul rises and falls and leaps and tumbles with you!
I shout aloud and incite you, O white-headed merry
    companions.
The sight of you alone is better than drinking.
The brazen band is loosened from off my forehead;
My breast and my brain are moistened and cool;   40
And still I yell in answer
To your hoarse inarticulate voices,
O big, strong, bullying, boisterous waves,
That are of all things in nature the nearest thoughts to human,
Because you are wicked and foolish,   45
Mad and destructive.

Stormy Nights

I cry out war to those who spend their utmost,
Trying to substitute a vain regret
For childhood's vanished moods,
Instead of a full manly satisfaction

In new development.   5
Their words are vain as the lost shouts,
The wasted breath of solitary hunters
That are far buried in primeval woods –
Clamour that dies in silence,
Cries that bring back no answer   10
But the great voice of the wind-shaken forest,
Mocking despair.

No – they will get no answer;
For I too recollect,
I recollect and love my perished childhood,   15
Perfectly love and keenly recollect;
I too remember; and if it could be
Would not recall it.

Do I not know, how, nightly, on my bed
The palpable close darkness shutting round me,   20
How my small heart went forth to evil things,
How all the possibilities of sin
That were yet present to my innocence
Bound me too narrowly,
And how my spirit beat   25
The cage of its compulsive purity;
How – my eyes fixed,
My shot lip tremulous between my fingers
I fashioned for myself new modes of crime,
Created for m) self with pain and labour   30
The evil that the cobwebs of society,
The comely secrecies of education,
Had made an itching mystery to meward.

Do I not know again,
When the great winds broke loose and went abroad   35
At night in the lighted town –
Ah! then it was different –
Then, when I seemed to hear
The storm go by me like a cloak-wrapt horseman
Stooping over the saddle –   40
Go by, and come again and yet again,

Like some one riding with a pardon,
And ever baffled, ever shut from passage:
Then when the house shook and a horde of noises
Came out and clattered over me all night,   45
Then, would my heart stand still,
My hair creep fearfully upon my head
And, with my tear-wet face
Buried among the bed-clothes,
Long and bitterly would I pray and wrestle   50
Till gentle sleep
Threw her great mantle over me,
And my hard breathing gradually ceased.

I was then the Indian,
Well and happy and full of glee and pleasure,   55
Both hands full of life.
And not without divine impulses
Shot into me by the untried non-ego;
But, like the Indian, too,
Not yet exempt from feverish questionings,   60
And on my bed of leaves,
Writhing terribly in grasp of terror,
As when the still stars and the great white moon
Watch me athwart black foliage,
Trembling before the interminable vista,   65
The widening wells of space
In which my thought flags like a wearied bird
In the mid ocean of his autumn flight –
Prostrate before the indefinite great spirit
That the external warder   70
Plunged like a dagger
Into my bosom.
Now, I am a Greek
White robed among the sunsh. ne and the statues
And the fair porticos of carven marble --   75
Fond of olives and dry sherry,
Good tobacco and clever talk with my fellows,
Free from inordinate cravings.
Why would you hurry me, O evangelist,
You with the bands and the shilling packet of tracts   80

Greatly reduced when taken for distribution?
Why do you taunt my progress,
O green-spectacled Wordsworth! in beautiful verses,
You, the elderly poet?
So I shall travel forward   85
Step by step with the rest of my race,
In time, if death should spare me,
I shall come on to a farther stage,
And show you St Francis of Assisi.

Song at Dawn

I see the dawn creep round the world,
Here damm'd a moment backward by great hills,
There racing o'er the sea.
Down at the round equator,
It leaps forth straight and rapid,   5
Driving with firm sharp edge the night before it.
Here gradually it floods
The wooded valleys and the weeds
And the still smokeless cities.
The cocks crow up at the farms;   10
The sick man's spirit is glad;
The watch treads brisker about the dew-wet deck;
The light-keeper locks his desk.
As the lenses turn,
Faded and yellow.   15

The girl with the embroidered shift
Rises and leans on the sill,
And her full bosom heaves
Drinking deep of the silentness.
I too rise and watch   20
The healing fingers of dawn –
I too drink from its eyes

The unaccountable peace –
I too drink and am satisfied as with food.
Fain would I go   25
Down by the winding crossroad by the trees,
Where at the corner of wet wood
The blackbird in the early grey and stillness
Wakes his first song.

Peace, who can make verses clink,
Find ictus following surely after ictus,
At such an hour as this, the heart
Lies steeped and silent.
O dreaming, leaning girl,
Already the grey passes, the white streak
Brightens above dark woodlands, Day begins.

To The Commissioners of Northern Lights, with a Paper

I send to you, commissioners,
A paper that may please ye, sirs,
(For troth they say it micht be worse
    An' I believ't)
And on your business lay my curse   5
    Before I leav't.

I thocht I'd serve wi' you, sirs, yince,
But I've thocht better of it since;
The maitter I will nowise mince,
    But tell ye true: 10
I'll service wi' some ither prince,
    An' no' wi' you.

I've no' been very deep, ye'll think,
Cam' delicately to the brink
An' when the water gart me shrink   15

      Straucht took the rue,
An' didna stoop my fill to drink –
      I own it true.

I kent on cape and isle, a light
Burnt fair an' clearly ilka night;   20
But at the service I took fright,
      As sune's I saw,
An' being still a neophite
      Gaed straucht awa'.

Anither course I now begin,   25
    The weeg I'll cairry for my sin,
    The court my voice sall echo in,
        An' – wha can tell? –
    Some ither day I may be yin
        O' you mysel'.   30

To Charles Baxter

Noo lyart leaves blaw ower the green,
Reid are the bonny woods o' Dean,
An' here we're back in Embro, frien',
    To pass the winter.
Whilk noo, wi' frosts afore, draws in,   5
    An' snaws ahint her.

I've seen 's hae days to fricht us a',
The Pentlands poothered weel wi' snaw,
The ways half smoored wi' liquid thaw
    An' half congealin',   10
The snell an' scowtherin' norther blaw
    Frae blae Brunteelan'.

I've seen 's been unco sweir to sally
And at the door-cheeks daff an' dally –

Seen 's daidle thus an' shilly-shally   15
    For near a minute –
Sae cauld the wind blew up the valley,
    The deil was in it! –

Syne spread the silk an' tak the gate,
In blast an' blaudin' rain, deil hae 't!   20
The hale toon glintin', stane an' slate,
    Wi' cauld an' weet,
An' to the Court, gin we 'se be late,
    Bicker oor feet.

And at the Court, tae, aft I saw   25
Whaur Advocates by twa an' twa
Gang gesterin' end to end the ha'
    In weeg an' goon,
To crack o' what ye wull but Law
    The hale forenoon.   30

That muckle ha', maist like a kirk,
I've kent at braid mid-day sae mirk
Ye'd seen white weegs an' faces lurk
    Like ghaists frae Hell,
But whether Christian ghaists or Turk   35
    Deil ane could tell.

The three fires lunted in the gloom,
The wind blew like the blast o' doom,
The rain upo' the roof abune
    Played Peter Dick –   40
Ye wad nae'd licht enough i' the room
    Your teeth to pick!

But, freend, ye ken how me an' you,
The ling-lang lanely winter through,
Keep'd a guid speerit up, an' true   45
    To lore Horatian,
We aye the ither bottle drew –
    To inclination.

Sae let us in the comin' days
Stand sicker on oor auncient ways –   50
The strauchtest road in a' the maze
        Since Eve ate apples;
An' let the winter weet oor cla'es –
        We'll weet oor thrapples.

from **Underwoods (1887)**

A Song of the Road

The gauger walked with willing foot,
And aye the gauger played the flute;
And what should Master Gauger play
But *Over the hills and far away?*

When'er I buckle on my pack   5
And foot it gaily in the track,
O pleasant gauger, long since dead,
I hear you fluting on ahead.

You go with me the self-same way –
The self-same air for me you play;   10
For I do think and so do you
It is the tune to travel to.

For who would gravely set his face
To go to this or t'other place?
There's nothing under Heav'n so blue   15
That's fairly worth the travelling to.

On every hand the roads begin,
And people walk with zeal therein;
But wheresoe'er the highways tend,
Be sure there's nothing at the end.   20

Then follow you, wherever hie
The travelling mountains of the sky.
Or let the streams in civil mode
Direct your choice upon a road;

For one and all, or high or low,   25
Will lead you where you wish to go;
  And one and all go night and day
  Over the hills and far away!

The House Beautiful

A naked house, a naked moor,
A shivering pool before the door,
A garden bare of flowers and fruit
And poplars at the garden foot:
Such is the place that I live in,   5
Bleak without and bare within.

Yet shall your ragged moor receive
The incomparable pomp of eve,
And the cold glories of the dawn
Behind your shivering trees be drawn;   10
And when the wind from place to place
Doth the unmoored cloud-galleons chase,
Your garden gloom and gleam again,
With leaping sun, with glancing rain.
Here shall the wizard moon ascend   15
The heavens, in the crimson end
Of day's declining splendour; here
The army of the stars appear.

The neighbour hollows dry or wet,
Spring shall with tender flowers beset;   20
And oft the morning muser see
Larks rising from the broomy lea,
And every fairy wheel and thread
Of cobweb dew-bediamonded.
When daisies go, shall winter time   25
Silver the simple grass with rime;
Autumnal frosts enchant the pool
And make the cart-ruts beautiful;
And when snow-bright the moor expands,
How shall your children clap their hands!   30
To make this earth, our hermitage,
A cheerful and a changeful page,
God's bright and intricate device
Of days and seasons doth suffice.

To Will H. Low

Youth now flees on feathered foot,
Faint and fainter sounds the flute,
Rarer songs of gods; and still
Somewhere on the sunny hill,
Or along the winding stream,   5
Through the willows, flits a dream;
Flits but shows a smiling face,
Flees but with so quaint a grace,
None can choose to stay at home,
All must follow, all must roam.   10

This is unborn beauty: she
Now in air floats high and free,
Takes the sun and breaks the blue; –
Late with stooping pinion flew
Raking hedgerow trees, and wet   15
Her wing in silver streams, and set
Shining foot on temple roof:
Now again she flies aloof,
Coasting mountain clouds and kiss't
By the evening's amethyst.   20

In wet wood and miry lane,
Still we pant and pound in vain;
Still with leaden foot we chase
Waning pinion, fainting face;
Still with gray hair we stumble on,   25
Till, behold, the vision gone!
Where hath fleeting beauty led?
To the doorway of the dead.
Life is over, life was gay:
We have come the primrose way.   30

To Mrs Will H. Low

Even in the bluest noonday of July,
There could not run the smallest breath of wind
But all the quarter sounded like a wood;
And in the chequered silence and above
The hum of city cabs that sought the Bois,   5
Suburban ashes shivered into song.
A patter and a chatter and a chirp
And a long dying hiss – it was as though
Starched old brocaded dames through all the house
Had trailed a strident skirt, or the whole sky   10
Even in a wink had over-brimmed in rain.
Hark, in these shady parlours, how it talks
Of the near Autumn, how the smitten ash
Trembles and augurs floods! O not too long
In these inconstant latitudes delay,   15
O not too late from the unbeloved north
Trim your escape! For soon shall this low roof
Resound indeed with rain, soon shall your eyes
Search the foul garden, search the darkened rooms,
Nor find one jewel but the blazing log.   20

To Andrew Lang

Dear Andrew, with the brindled hair,
Who glory to have thrown in air,
High over arm, the trembling reed,
By Ale and Kail, by Till and Tweed:
An equal craft of hand you show   5
The pen to guide, the fly to throw:
I count you happy starred; for God,
When He with inkpot and with rod
Endowed you, bade your fortune lead
Forever by the crooks of Tweed,   10

Forever by the woods of song
And lands that to the Muse belong;
Or if in peopled streets, or in
The abhorred pedantic sanhedrin,
It should be yours to wander, still   15
Airs of the morn, airs of the hill,
The plovery Forest and the seas
That break about the Hebrides,
Should follow over field and plain
And find you at the window pane;   20
And you again see hill and peel,
And the bright springs gush at your heel.
So went the fiat forth, and so
Garrulous like a brook you go,
With sound of happy mirth and sheen   25
Of daylight – whether by the green
You fare that moment, or the gray;
Whether you dwell in March or May;
Or whether treat of reels and rods
Or of the old unhappy gods: 30
Still like a brook your page has shone,
And your ink sings of Helicon.

To W. E. Henley

The year runs through her phases; rain and sun,
Springtime and summer pass; winter succeeds;
But one pale season rules the house of death.
Cold falls the imprisoned daylight; fell disease
By each lean pallet squats, and pain and sleep   5
Toss gaping on the pillows.
                              But O thou!
Uprise and take thy pipe. Bid music flow,
Strains by good thoughts attended, like the spring
The swallows follow over land and sea.   10
Pain sleeps at once; at once, with open eyes,

Dozing despair awakes. The shepherd sees
His flock come bleating home; the seaman hears
Once more the cordage rattle. Airs of home!
Youth, love and roses blossom; the gaunt ward   15
Dislimns and disappears, and, opening out,
Shows brooks and forests, and the blue beyond
Of mountains.
           Small the pipe; but O! do thou,
Peak-faced and suffering piper, blow therein   20
The dirge of heroes dead; and to these sick,
These dying, sound the triumph over death.
Behold! each greatly breathes; each tastes a joy
Unknown before, in dying; for each knows
A hero dies with him – though unfulfilled,   25
Yet conquering truly – and not dies in vain.

So is pain cheered, death comforted; the house
Of sorrow smiles to listen. Once again –
O thou, Orpheus and Heracles, the bard
And the deliverer, touch the stops again!   30

Henry James

Who comes tonight? We ope the doors in vain.
Who comes? My bursting walls, can you contain
The presences that now together throng
Your narrow entry, as with flowers and song,
As with the air of life, the breath of talk?   5
Lo, how these fair immaculate women walk
Behind their jocund maker; and we see
Slighted *De Mauves*, and that far different she,
Gressie, the trivial sphinx; and to our feast
Daisy and *Barb* and *Chancellor* (she not least!)   10
With all their silken, all their airy kin,
Do like unbidden angels enter in.
But he, attended by these shining names,
Comes (best of all) himself – our welcome James.

The Mirror Speaks

Where the bells peal far at sea
Cunning fingers fashioned me.
There on palace walls I hung
While that Consuelo sung;
But I heard, though I listened well,   5
Never a note, never a trill,
Never a beat of the chiming bell.
There I hung and looked, and there
In my gray face, faces fair
Shone from under shining hair.   10
Well I saw the poising head,
But the lips moved and nothing said;
And when lights were in the hall,
Silent moved the dancers all.

So awhile I glowed, and then   15
Fell on dusty days and men;
Long I slumbered packed in straw,
Long I none but dealers saw;
Till before my silent eye
One that sees came passing by.   20

Now with an outlandish grace,
To the sparkling fire I face
In the blue room at Skerryvore;
Where I wait until the door
Open, and the Prince of Men,   25
Henry James, shall come again.

Requiem

Under the wide and starry sky,
Dig the grave and let me lie.
Glad did I live and gladly die,
   And I laid me down with a will.

This be the verse you grave for me: 5
Here he lies where he longed to be;
Home is the sailor, home from sea,
   And the hunter home from the hill.

The Celestial Surgeon

If I have faltered more or less
In my great task of happiness;
If I have moved among my race
And shown no glorious morning face;
If beams from happy human eyes   5
Have moved me not; if morning skies,
Books, and my food, and summer rain
Knocked on my sullen heart in vain:
Lord, thy most pointed pleasure take
And stab my spirit broad awake;   10
Or, Lord, if too obdurate I,
Choose thou, before that spirit die,
A piercing pain, a killing sin,
And to my dead heart run them in!

In Memoriam F. A. S.

Yet, O stricken heart, remember, O remember
  How of human days he lived the better part.
April came to bloom and never dim December
  Breathed its killing chills upon the head or heart.

Doomed to know not Winter, only Spring, a being   5
  Trod the flowery April blithely for a while,
Took his fill of music, joy of thought and seeing,
  Came and stayed and went, nor ever ceased to smile.

Came and stayed and went, and now when all is finished,
  You alone have crossed the melancholy stream,   10
Yours the pang, but his, O his, the undiminished
  Undecaying gladness, undeparted dream.

All that life contains of torture, toil, and treason,
  Shame, dishonour, death, to him were but a name.
Here, a boy, he dwelt through all the singing season   15
  And ere the day of sorrow departed as he came.

To My Father

Peace and her huge invasion to these shores
Puts daily home; innumerable sails
Dawn on the far horizon and draw near;
Innumerable loves, uncounted hopes
To our wild coasts, not darkling now, approach: 5
Not now obscure, since thou and thine are there,
And bright on the lone isle, the foundered reef,
The long, resounding foreland, Pharos stands.

These are thy works, O father, these thy crown;
Whether on high the air be pure, they shine   10

Along the yellowing sunset, and all night
Among the unnumbered stars of God they shine;
Or whether fogs arise and far and wide
The low sea-level drown – each finds a tongue
And all night long the tolling bell resounds: 15
So shine, so toll, till night be overpast,
Till the star vanish, till the sun return,
And in the haven rides the fleet secure.

In the first hour, the seaman in his skiff
Moves through the unmoving bay, to where the town   20
Its earliest smoke into the air upbreathes
And the rough hazels climb along the beach.
To the tugg'd oar the distant echo speaks.
The ship lies resting, where by reef and roost
Thou and thy lights have led her like a child.   25

This hast thou done, and I – can I be base?
I must arise, O father, and to port
Some lost, complaining seaman pilot home.

A Portrait

I am a kind of farthing dip,
    Unfriendly to the nose and eyes;
A blue-behinded ape, I skip
    Upon the trees of Paradise.

At mankind's feast, I take my place   5
    In solemn, sanctimonious state,
And have the air of saying grace
    While I defile the dinner plate.

I am 'the smiler with the knife',
    The battener upon garbage, I –   10
Dear Heaven, with such a rancid life,
    Were it not better far to die?

Yet still, about the human pale,
   I love to scamper, love to race,
To swing by my irreverent tail   15
   All over the most holy place;

And when at length, some golden day,
   The unfailing sportsman, aiming at,
Shall bag, me – all the world shall say:
   Thank God, and there's an end of that!   20

A Camp

The bed was made, the room was fit,
By punctual eve the stars were lit;
The air was still, the water ran,
No need was there for maid or man,
When we put up, my ass and I,   5
At God's green caravanserai.

The Country of the Camisards

We travelled in the print of olden wars,
   Yet all the land was green,
   And love we found, and peace,
   Where fire and war had been.

They pass and smile, the children of the sword –   5
   No more the sword they wield;
   And O, how deep the corn
   Along the battlefield!

Skerryvore

For love of lovely words, and for the sake
Of those, my kinsmen and my countrymen,
Who early and late in the windy ocean toiled
To plant a star for seamen, where was then
The surfy haunt of seals and cormorants: 5
I, on the lintel of this cot, inscribe
The name of a strong tower.

Skerryvore: The Parallel

Here all is sunny, and when the truant gull
Skims the green level of the lawn, his wing
Dispetals roses; here the house is framed
Of kneaded brick and the plumed mountain pine,
Such clay as artists fashion and such wood   5
As the tree-climbing urchin breaks. But there
Eternal granite hewn from the living isle
And dowelled with brute iron, rears a tower
That from its wet foundation to its crown
Of glittering glass, stands, in the sweep of winds,   10
Immovable, immortal, eminent.

My House, I say . . .

My house, I say. But hark to the sunny doves
That make my roof the arena of their loves,
That gyre about the gable all day long
And fill the chimneys with their murmurous song:
Our house, they say; and *mine*, the cat declares   5

And spreads his golden fleece upon the chairs;
And *mine* the dog, and rises stiff with wrath
If any alien foot profane the path.
So too the buck that trimmed my terraces,
Our whilome gardener, called the garden his;   10
Who now, deposed, surveys my plain abode
And his late kingdom, only from the road.

Say not of me . . .

Say not of me that weakly I declined
The labours of my sires, and fled the sea,
The towers we founded and the lamps we lit,
To play at home with paper like a child.
But rather say: *In the afternoon of time*   5
A strenuous family dusted from its hands
The sand of granite, and beholding far
Along the sounding coast its pyramids
And tall memorials catch the dying sun,
Smiled well content, and to this childish task   10
Around the fire addressed its evening hours.

The Maker to Posterity

Far 'yont amang the years to be
When a' we think, an' a' we see,
An' a' we luve, 's been dung ajee
          By time's rouch shouther,
An' what was richt and wrang for me   5
          Lies mangled throu'ther,

It's possible – it's hardly mair –
That some ane, ripin' after lear –

Some auld professor or young heir,
    If still there's either –   10
May find an' read me, an' be sair
    Perplexed, puir brither!

'*What tongue does your auld bookie speak?*'
He'll spier; an' I, his mou to steik:
'*No bein' fit to write in Greek,*   15
    I wrote in Lallan,
Dear to my heart as the peat reek,
    Auld as Tantallon.

'*Few spak it than, an' noo there's nane.*
My puir auld sangs lie a' their lane,   20
Their sense, that aince was braw an' plain,
    Tint a'thegether,
Like runes upon a standin' stane
    Amang the heather.

'*But think not you the brae to speel;*   25
You, tae, maun chow the bitter peel;
For a' your lear, for a' your skeel,
    Ye're nane sae lucky;
An' things are mebbe waur than weel
    For you, my buckie.   30

'*The hale concern (baith hens an' eggs,*
Baith books an' writers, stars an' clegs)
Noo stachers upon lowsent legs
    An' wears awa';
The tack o' mankind, near the dregs,   35
    Rins unco' law.

'*Your book, that in some braw new tongue,*
Ye wrote or prentit, preached or sung,
Will still be just a bairn, an' young
    In fame an' years,
Whan the hale planet's guts are dung   40
    About your ears;

'An' you, sair gruppin' to a spar
Or whammled wi' some bleezin' star,
Cryin' to ken whaur deil ye are,   45
        Hame, France, or Flanders –
Whang sindry like a railway car
        An' flie in danders.'

Ille Terrarum

Frae nirly, nippin', Eas'lan' breeze,
Frae Norlan' snaw, an' haar o' seas,
Weel happit in your gairden trees,
        A bonny bit,
Atween the muckly Pentland's knees,   5
        Secure ye sit.

Beeches an' aiks entwine their theek,
An' firs, a stench, auld-farrant clique.
A' simmer day, your chimleys reek,
        Couthy and bien;   10
An' here an' there your windies keek
        Amang the green.

A pickle plats an' paths an' posies,
A wheen auld gillyflowers an' roses:
A ring o' wa's the hale encloses   15
        Frae sheep or men;
An' there the auld housie beeks an' dozes,
        A' by her lane.

The gairdner crooks his weary back
A' day in the pitaty-track,   20
Or mebbe stops awhile to crack
        Wi' Jane the cook,
Or at some buss, worm-eaten-black,
        To gie a look.

Frae the high hills the curlew ca's;   25
The sheep gang baaing by the wa's;
Or whiles a clan o' roosty craws
    Cangle thegether;
The wild bees seek the gairden raws,
    Weariet wi' heather.   30

Or in the gloamin' douce an' gray
The sweet-throat mavis tunes her lay;
The herd comes likin' doun the brae;
    An' by degrees
The muckle siller müne maks way   35
    Amang the trees.

Here aft hae I, wi' sober heart,
For meditation sat apairt,
When orra loves or kittle art
    Perplexed my mind;   40
Here socht a balm for ilka smart
    O' humankind.

Here aft, weel neukit by my lane,
Wi' Horace, or perhaps Montaigne,
The mornin' hours hae come an' gane   45
    Abüne my heid –
I wadnae gi'en a chucky-stane
    For a' I'd read.

But noo the auld city, street by street,
An' winter fu' o' snaw an' sleet,   50
Awhile shut in my gangrel feet
    An' goavin' mettle;
Noo is the soopit ingle sweet,
    An' liltin' kettle.

An' noo the winter winds complain;   55
Cauld lies the glaur in ilka lane;
On draigled hizzie, tautit wean
    An' drucken lads,

In the mirk nicht, the winter rain
  Dribbles an' blads.   60

Whan bugles frae the Castle rock,
An' beaten drums wi' dowie shock,
Wauken, at cauld-rife sax o'clock,
  My chitterin' frame,
I mind me on the kintry cock,   65
  The kintry hame.

I mind me on yon bonny bield;
An' Fancy traivels far afield
To gaither a' that gairdens yield
  O' sun an' Simmer: 70
To hearten up a dowie chield,
  Fancy's the limmer!

A Mile an' a Bittock

A mile an' a bittock, a mile or twa,
Abüne the burn, ayont the law,
Davie an' Donal' an' Cherlie an' a',
  An' the müne was shinin' clearly!

Ane went hame wi' the ither, an' then 5
The ither went hame wi' the ither twa men,
An' baith wad return him the service again,
  An' the müne was shinin' clearly!

The clocks were chappin' in house an' ha',
Eleeven, twal an' ane an' twa;   10
An' the guidman's face was turnt to the wa',
  An' the müne was shinin' clearly!

A wind got up frae affa the sea,
It blew the stars as clear's could be,

It blew in the een of a' o' the three,   15
    An' the müne was shinin' clearly!

Noo, Davie was first to get sleep in his head,
'The best o' frien's maun twine,' he said;
'I'm weariet, an' here I'm awa' to my bed.'
    An' the müne was shinin' clearly!   20

Twa o' them walkin' an' crackin' their lane,
The mornin' licht cam gray an' plain,
An' the birds they yammert on stick an' stane,
    An' the müne was shinin' clearly!

O years ayont, O years awa',   25
My lads, ye'll mind whate'er befa' –
My lads, ye'll mind on the bield o' the law,
    When the müne was shinin' clearly.

A Lowden Sabbath Morn

The clinkum-clank o' Sabbath bells
Noo to the hoastin' rookery swells,
Noo faintin' laigh in shady dells,
    Sounds far an' near,
An' through the simmer kintry tells   5
    Its tale o' cheer.

An' noo, to that melodious play,
A' deidly awn the quiet sway –
A' ken their solemn holiday,
    Bestial an' human,   10
The singin' lintie on the brae,
    The restin' plou'man.

He, mair than a' the lave o' men,
His week completit joys to ken;
Half-dressed, he daunders out an' in,   15

Perplext wi' leisure;
An' his raxt limbs he'll rax again
Wi' painfu' pleesure.

The steerin' mither strange afit
Noo shoos the bairnies but a bit;   20
Noo cries them ben, their Sinday shüit
        To scart upon them,
Or sweeties in their pouch to pit,
        Wi' blessin's on them.

The lasses, clean frae tap to taes,   25
Are busked in crunklin' underclaes;
The gartened hose, the weel-filled stays,
        The nakit shift,
A' bleached on bonny greens for days,
        An' white's the drift.   30

An' noo to face the kirkward mile:
The guidman's hat o' dacent style,
The blackit shoon, we noo maun fyle
        As white's the miller:
A waefü' peety tae, to spile   35
        The warth o' siller.

Our Marg'et, aye sae keen to crack,
Douce-stappin' in the stoury track,
Her emeralt goun a' kiltit back
        Frae snawy coats,   40
White-ankled, leads the kirkward pack
        Wi' Dauvit Groats.

A thocht ahint, in runkled breeks,
A' spiled wi' lyin' by for weeks,
The guidman follows closs, an' cleiks   45
        The sonsie missis;
His sarious face at aince bespeaks
        The day that this is.

And aye an' while we nearer draw
To whaur the kirkton lies alaw,   50

Mair neebours, comin' saft an' slaw
     Frae here an' there,
The thicker thrang the gate an' caw
     The stour in air.

But hark! the bells frae nearer clang;   55
To rowst the slaw, their sides they bang;
An' see! black coats a'ready thrang
     The green kirkyaird;
And at the yett, the chestnuts sprang
     That brocht the laird.   60

The solemn elders at the plate
Stand drinkin' deep the pride o' state:
The practised hands as gash an' great
     As Lords o' Session;
The later named, a wee thing blate   65
     In their expression.

The prentit stanes that mark the deid,
Wi' lengthened lip, the sarious read;
Syne wag a moraleesin' heid,
     An' then an' there
Their hirplin' practice an' their creed   70
     Try hard to square.

It's here our Merren lang has lain,
A wee bewast the table-stane;
An' yon's the grave o' Sandy Blane;   75
     An' further ower,
The mither's brithers, dacent men!
     Lie a' the fower.

Here the guidman sall bide awee
To dwall amang the deid; to see   80
Auld faces clear in fancy's e'e;
     Belike to hear
Auld voices fa'in saft an' slee
     On fancy's ear.

Thus, on the day o' solemn things,   85
The bell that in the steeple swings
To fauld a scaittered faim'ly rings
        Its walcome screed;
An' just a wee thing nearer brings
        The quick an' deid.   90

But noo the bell is ringin' in;
To tak their places, folk begin;
The minister himsel' will shüne
        Be up the gate,
Filled fu' wi' clavers about sin   95
        An' man's estate.

The tünes are up – *French*, to be shüre,
The faithfü' *French*, an' twa-three mair;
The auld prezentor, hoastin' sair,
        Wales out the portions,   100
An' yirks the tüne into the air
        Wi' queer contortions.

Follow the prayer, the readin' next,
An' than the fisslin' for the text –
The twa-three last to find it, vext   105
        But kind o' proud;
An' than the peppermints are raxed,
        An' southernwood.

For noo's the time whan pows are seen
Nid noddin' like a mandareen;   110
When tenty mithers stap a preen
        In sleepin' weans;
An' nearly half the parochine
        Forget their pains.

There's just a waukrif' twa or three: 115
Thrawn commentautors sweet to 'gree,
Weans glowrin' at the bumlin' bee
        On windie-glasses,
Or lads that tak a keek a-glee
        At sonsie lasses.   120

Himsel', meanwhile, frae whaur he cocks
An' bobs belaw the soundin'-box,
The treesures of his words unlocks
    Wi' prodigality,
An' deals some unco dingin' knocks   125
    To infidality.

Wi' sappy unction, hoo he burkes
The hopes o' men that trust in works,
Expounds the fau'ts o' ither kirks,
    An' shaws the best o' them   130
No muckle better than mere Turks,
    When a's confessed o' them.

Bethankit! what a bonny creed!
What mair would ony Christian need? –
The braw words rumm'le ower his heid,   135
    Nor steer the sleeper;
And in their restin' graves, the deid
    Sleep aye the deeper.

The Spaewife

O, I wad like to ken – to the beggar-wife says I –
Why chops are guid to brander and nane sae guid to fry.
An' siller, that's sae braw to keep, is brawer still to gi'e.
– *It's gey an' easy spierin'*, says the beggar-wife to me.

O, I wad like to ken – to the beggar-wife says I –   5
Hoo a' things come to be whaur we find them when we try,
The lasses in their claes an' the fishes in the sea.
– *It's gey an' easy spierin'*, says the beggar-wife to me.

O, I wad like to ken – to the beggar-wife says I –
Why lads are a' to sell an' lasses a' to buy;   10

An' naebody for dacency but barely twa or three.
– *It's gey an' easy spierin'*, says the beggar-wife to me.

O, I wad like to ken – to the beggar-wife says I –
Gin death's as shüre to men as killin' is to kye,
Why God has filled the yearth sae fu' o' tasty things to pree.   15
– *It's gey an' easy spierin'*, says the beggar-wife to me.

O, I wad like to ken – to the beggar wife says I –
The reason o' the cause an' the wherefore o' the why,
Wi' mony anither riddle brings the tears into my e'e.
– *It's gey an' easy spierin'*, says the beggar-wife to me.   20

My Conscience!

Of a' the ills that flesh can fear,
The loss o' frien's, the lack o' gear,
A yowlin' tyke, a glandered mear,
          A lassie's nonsense –
There's just ae thing I cannae bear,   5
          An' that's my conscience.

Whan day (an' a' excüse) has gane,
An' wark is düne, and duty's plain,
An' to my chalmer a' my lane
          I creep apairt,   10
My conscience! hoo the yammerin' pain
          Stends to my heart!

An' day wi' various ends in view
The hairsts o' time I had to pu',
An' made a hash wad staw a soo,   15
          Let be a man! –
My conscience! whan my han's were fu',
          Whaur were ye than?

An' there were a' the lures o' life,
There pleesure skirlin' on the fife,   20
There anger, wi' the hotchin' knife
          Ground shairp in Hell –
My conscience! – you that's like a wife! –
          Whaur was yoursel'?

I ken it fine: just waitin' here,   25
To gar the evil waur appear,
To clart the guid, confüse the clear,
          Mis-ca' the great,
My conscience! an' to raise a steer
          Whan a's ower late.   30

Sic-like, some tyke grawn auld and blind,
Whan thieves brok' through the gear to p'ind,
Has lain his dozened length an' grinned
          At the disaster;
An' the morn's mornin', wud's the wind,   35
          Yokes on his master.

from **A Child's Garden of Verses (1885)**

Pirate Story

Three of us afloat in the meadow by the swing,
   Three of us aboard in the basket on the lea.
Winds are in the air, they are blowing in the spring,
   And waves are on the meadow like the waves there are at sea.

Where shall we adventure, today that we're afloat,   5
   Wary of the weather and steering by a star?
Shall it be to Africa, a-steering of the boat,
   To Providence, or Babylon, or off to Malabar?

Hi! but here's a squadron a-rowing on the sea –
   Cattle on the meadow a-charging with a roar!   10
Quick, and we'll escape them, they're as mad as they can be,
   The wicket is the harbour and the garden is the shore.

Windy Nights

Whenever the moon and stars are set,
   Whenever the wind is high,
All night long in the dark and wet,
   A man goes riding by.
Late in the night when the fires are out,   5
Why does he gallop and gallop about?

Whenever the trees are crying aloud,
   And ships are tossed at sea,
By, on the highway, low and loud,
   By at the gallop goes he.   10

By at the gallop he goes, and then
By he comes back at the gallop again.

Travel

I should like to rise and go
Where the golden apples grow;
Where below another sky
Parrot islands anchored lie,
And, watched by cockatoos and goats,   5
Lonely Crusoes building boats;
Where in sunshine reaching out
Eastern cities, miles about,
Are with mosque and minaret
Among sandy gardens set,   10
And the rich goods from near and far
Hang for sale in the bazaar;
Where the Great Wall round China goes,
And on one side the desert blows,
And with bell and voice and drum,   15
Cities on the other hum;
Where are forests, hot as fire,
Wide as England, tall as a spire,
Full of apes and cocoa-nuts
And the negro hunters' huts;   20
Where the knotty crocodile
Lies and blinks in the Nile,
And the red flamingo flies
Hunting fish before his eyes;
Where in jungles, near and far,   25
Man-devouring tigers are,
Lying close and giving ear
Lest the hunt be drawing near,
Or a comer-by be seen
Swinging in a palanquin;   30

Where among the desert sands
Some deserted city stands,
All its children, sweep and prince,
Grown to manhood ages since,
Not a foot in street or house,   35
Not a stir of child or mouse,
And when kindly falls the night,
In all the town no spark of light.
There I'll come when I'm a man
With a camel caravan;   40
Light a fire in the gloom
Of some dusty dining-room;
See the pictures on the walls,
Heroes, fights and festivals;
And in a corner find the toys   45
Of the old Egyptian boys.

Where Go the Boats?

Dark brown is the river,
    Golden is the sand.
It flows along for ever,
    With trees on either hand.

Green leaves a-floating,   5
    Castles of the foam,
Boats of mine a-boating –
    Where will all come home?

On goes the river
    And out past the mill,   10
Away down the valley,
    Away down the hill.

Away down the river,
   A hundred miles or more,
Other little children   15
   Shall bring my boats ashore.

The Land of Counterpane

When I was sick and lay a-bed,
I had two pillows at my head,
And all my toys beside me lay
To keep me happy all the day.

And sometimes for an hour or so   5
I watched my leaden soldiers go,
With different uniforms and drills,
Among the bed-clothes, through the hills;

And sometimes sent my ships in fleets
All up and down among the sheets;   10
Or brought my trees and houses out,
And planted cities all about.

I was the giant great and still
That sits upon the pillow-hill,
And sees before him, dale and plain,   15
The pleasant land of counterpane.

My Shadow

I have a little shadow that goes in and out with me,
And what can be the use of him is more than I can see.
He is very, very like me from the heels up to the head;
And I see him jump before me, when I jump into my bed.

The funniest thing about him is the way he likes to grow —   5
Not at all like proper children, which is always very slow;
For he sometimes shoots up taller like an india-rubber ball,
And he sometimes gets so little that there's none of him at all.

He hasn't got a notion of how children ought to play,
And can only make a fool of me in every sort of way.   10
He stays so close beside me, he's a coward you can see;
I'd think shame to stick to nursie as that shadow sticks to me!

One morning, very early, before the sun was up,
I rose and found the shining dew on every buttercup;
But my lazy little shadow, like an arrant sleepy-head,   15
Had stayed at home behind me and was fast asleep in bed.

Happy Thought

The world is so full of a number of things,
I'm sure we should all be as happy as kings.

Keepsake Mill

Over the borders, a sin without pardon,
   Breaking the branches and crawling below,
Out through the breach in the wall of the garden,
   Down by the banks of the river, we go.

Here is the mill with the humming of thunder,   5
   Here is the weir with the wonder of foam,
Here is the sluice with the race running under –
   Marvellous places, though handy to home!

Sounds of the village grow stiller and stiller,
   Stiller the note of the birds on the hill;   10
Dusty and dim are the eyes of the miller,
   Deaf are his ears with the moil of the mill.

Years may go by, and the wheel in the river
   Wheel as it wheels for us, children, today,
Wheel and keep roaring and foaming for ever   15
   Long after all of the boys are away.

Home from the Indies and home from the ocean,
   Heroes and soldiers we all shall come home;
Still we shall find the old mill wheel in motion,
   Turning and churning that river to foam.   20

You with the bean that I gave when we quarrelled,
   I with your marble of Saturday last,
Honoured and old and all gaily apparelled,
   Here we shall meet and remember the past.

The Lamplighter

My tea is nearly ready and the sun has left the sky;
It's time to take the window to see Leerie going by;
For every night at teatime and before you take your seat,
With lantern and with ladder he comes posting up the street.

Now Tom would be a driver and Maria go to sea,   5
And my papa's a banker and as rich as he can be;
But I, when I am stronger and can choose what I'm to do,
O Leerie, I'll go round at night and light the lamps with you!

For we are very lucky, with a lamp before the door,
And Leerie stops to light it as he lights so many more;   10
And O! before you hurry by with ladder and with light,
O Leerie, see a little child and nod to him tonight!

From a Railway Carriage

Faster than fairies, faster than witches,
Bridges and houses, hedges and ditches;
And charging along like troops in a battle,
All through the meadows the horses and cattle:
All of the sights of the hill and the plain   5
Fly as thick as driving rain;
And ever again, in the wink of an eye,
Painted stations whistle by.

Here is a child who clambers and scrambles,
All by himself and gathering brambles;   10
Here is a tramp who stands and gazes;
And there is the green for stringing the daisies!
Here is a cart run away in the road
Lumping along with man and load;

And here is a mill and there is a river: 15
Each a glimpse and gone for ever!

North-West Passage

1 GOOD NIGHT

When the bright lamp is carried in,
The sunless hours again begin;
O'er all without, in field and lane,
The haunted night returns again.

Now we behold the embers flee   5
About the firelit hearth; and see
Our faces painted as we pass,
Like pictures, on the window-glass.

Must we to bed indeed? Well then,
Let us arise and go like men,   10
And face with an undaunted tread
The long black passage up to bed.

Farewell, O brother, sister, sire!
O pleasant party round the fire?
The songs you sing, the tales you tell,   15
Till far tomorrow, fare ye well!

2 SHADOW MARCH

All round the house is the jet-black night;
    It stares through the window-pane;
It crawls in the corners, hiding from the light,
    And it moves with the moving flame.   20

Now my little heart goes a-beating like a drum,
    With the breath of the Bogie in my hair;
And all round the candle the crooked shadows come
    And go marching along up the stair.

The shadow of the balusters, the shadow of the lamp,   25
    The shadow of the child that goes to bed –
All the wicked shadows coming, tramp, tramp, tramp,
    With the black night overhead.

3 IN PORT

Last, to the chamber where I lie
My fearful footsteps patter nigh,   30
And come from out the cold and gloom
Into my warm and cheerful room.

There, safe arrived, we turn about
To keep the coming shadows out,
And close the happy door at last   35
On all the perils that we past.

Then, when mamma goes by to bed,
She shall come in with tip-toe tread,
And see me lying warm and fast
And in the Land of Nod at last.   40

To My Name-Child

1

Some day soon this rhyming volume, if you learn with proper
    speed,
Little Louis Sanchez, will be given you to read.
Then shall you discover that your name was printed down
By the English printers, long before, in London town.

In the great and busy city where the East and West are met,   5
    All the little letters did the English printer set;
    While you thought of nothing, and were still too young to
    play,
Foreign people thought of you in places far away.

Ay, and while you slept, a baby, over all the English lands
    Other little children took the volume in their hands;   10
Other children questioned, in their homes across the seas:
Who was little Louis, won't you tell us, mother, please?

2

Now that you have spelt your lesson, lay it down and go and
    play,
Seeking shells and seaweed on the sands of Monterey,
Watching all the mighty whalebones, lying buried by the
    breeze,   15
Tiny sandy-papers, and the huge Pacific seas.

And remember in your playing, as the sea-fog rolls to you,
Long ere you could read it, how I told you what to do;
And that while you thought of no one, nearly half the world
    away
Some one thought of Louis on the beach of Monterey!   20

To Any Reader

    As from the house your mother sees
    You playing round the garden trees,
    So you may see, if you will look
    Through the windows of this book,
    Another child, far, far away,   5
    And in another garden, play.
    But do not think you can at all,
    By knocking on the window, call
    That child to hear you. He intent
    Is all on his play-business bent.   10
    He does not hear; he will not look,
    Nor yet be lured out of this book.

For, long ago, the truth to say,
He has grown up and gone away,
And it is but a child of air 15
That lingers in the garden there.

from **Ballads (1890)**

from The Song of Rahéro

A Legend of Tahiti

2   THE VENGING OF TÁMATÉA

Thus was Rahéro's treason; thus and no further it sped.
The king sat safe in his place and a kindly fool was dead.

But the mother of Támatéa arose with death in her eyes.
All night long, and the next, Taiárapu rang with her cries.   185
As when a babe in the wood turns with a chill of doubt
And perceives nor home, nor friends, for the trees have
    closed her about,
The mountain rings and her breast is torn with the voice of
    despair:
So the lion-like woman idly wearied the air
For awhile, and pierced men's hearing in vain, and
    wounded their hearts.   190
But as when the weather changes at sea, in dangerous
    parts,
And sudden the hurricane wrack unrolls up the front of the
    sky,
At once the ship lies idle, the sails hang silent on high,
The breath of the wind that blew is blown out like the flame
    of a lamp,
And the silent armies of death draw near with inaudible
    tramp: 195
So sudden, the voice of her weeping ceased; in silence she
    rose
And passed from the house of her sorrow, a woman clothed
    with repose,
Carrying death in her breast and sharpening death with her
    hand.

Hither she went and thither in all the coasts of the land.

They tell that she feared not to slumber alone, in the dead
    of night,   200
In accursed places; beheld, unblenched, the ribbon of light
Spin from temple to temple; guided the perilous skiff,
Abhorred not the paths of the mountain and trod the verge
    of the cliff;
From end to end of the island, thought not the distance
    long,
But forth from king to king carried the tale of her wrong.   205
To king after king, as they sat in the palace door, she came,
Claiming kinship, declaiming verses, naming her name
And the names of all of her fathers; and still, with a heart
    on the rack,
Jested to capture a hearing and laughed when they jested
    back:
So would deceive them awhile, and change and return in a
    breath,   210
And on all the men of Vaiau imprecate instant death;
And tempt her kings – for Vaiau was a rich and prosperous
    land,
And flatter – for who would attempt it but warriors mighty
    of hand?
And change in a breath again and rise in a strain of song,
Invoking the beaten drums, beholding the fall of the strong,   215
Calling the fowls of the air to come and feast on the dead.
And they held the chin in silence, and heard her, and shook
    the head;
For they knew the men of Taiárapu famous in battle and
    feast,
Marvellous eaters and smiters: the man of Vaiau not least.

To the land of the Námunu-úra, to Paea, at length she
    came,   220
To men who were foes to the Tevas and hated their race
    and name,
There was she well received, and spoke with Hiopa the
    king.
And Hiopa listened, and weighed, and wisely considered the
    thing.
'Here in the back of the isle we dwell in a sheltered place,'

Quoth he to the woman, 'in quiet, a weak and peaceable
   race.   225
But far in the teeth of the wind lofty Taiárapu lies;
Strong blows the wind of the trade on its seaward face, and
   cries
Aloud in the top of arduous mountains, and utters its song
In green continuous forests. Strong is the wind, and strong
And fruitful and hardy the race, famous in battle and feast,   230
Marvellous eaters and smiters: the men of Vaiau not least.
Now hearken to me, my daughter, and hear a word of the
   wise:
How a strength goes linked with a weakness, two by two,
   like the eyes.
They can wield the ómare well and cast the javelin far;
Yet are they greedy and weak as the swine and the children
   are.   235
Plant we, then, here at Paea, a garden of excellent fruits;
Plant we bananas and kava and taro, the king of roots;
Let the pigs in Paea be tapu and no man fish for a year;
And of all the meat in Tahiti gather we threefold here.
So shall the fame of our plenty fill the island, and so,   240
At last, on the tongue of rumour, go where we wish it to
   go.
Then shall the pigs of Taiárapu raise their snouts in the air;
But we sit quiet and wait, as the fowler sits by the snare,
And tranquilly fold our hands, till the pigs come nosing the
   food:
But meanwhile build us a house of Trotéa, the stubborn
   wood,   245
Bind it with incombustible thongs, set a roof to the room,
Too strong for the hands of a man to dissever or fire to
   consume;
And there, when the pigs come trotting, there shall the
   feast be spread,
There shall the eye of the morn enlighten the feasters dead.
So be it done; for I have a heart that pities your state,   250
And Nateva and Námunu-úra are fire and water for hate.'

All was done as he said, and the gardens prospered; and
   now

The fame of their plenty went out, and word of it came to
    Vaiau.
For the men of Námunu-úra sailed, to the windward far,
Lay in the offing by south where the towns of the Tevas are,   255
And cast overboard of their plenty; and lo! at the Tevas' feet
The surf on all of the beaches tumbled treasures of meat.
In the salt of the sea, a harvest tossed with the refluent
    foam;
And the children gleaned it in playing, and ate and carried
    it home;
And the elders stared and debated, and wondered and
    passed the jest,   260
But whenever a guest came by eagerly questioned the
    guest;
And little by little, from one to another, the word went
    round:
'In all the borders of Paea the victual rots on the ground,
And swine are plenty as rats. And now, when they fare to
    the sea,
The men of the Námunu-úra glean from under the tree   265
And load the canoe to the gunwale with all that is
    toothsome to eat;
And all day long on the sea the jaws are crushing the meat,
The steersman eats at the helm, the rowers munch at the
    oar,
And at length, when their bellies are full, overboard with
    the store!'
Now was the word made true, and soon as the bait was
    bare,   270
All the pigs of Taiárapu raised their snouts in the air.
Songs were recited, and kinship was counted, and tales
    were told
How war had severed of late but peace had cemented of old
The clans of the island. 'To war,' said they, 'now set we an
    end,
And hie to the Námunu-úra even as a friend to a friend.'   275

So judged, and a day was named; and soon as the morning
    broke,
Canoes were thrust in the sea and the houses emptied of
    folk.

Strong blew the wind of the south, the wind that gathers
   the clan;
Along all the line of the reef the clamorous surges ran;
And the clouds were piled on the top of the island
   mountain-high,   280
A mountain throned on a mountain. The fleet of canoes
   swept by
In the midst, on the green lagoon, with a crew released
   from care,
Sailing an even water, breathing a summer air,
Cheered by a cloudless sun; and ever to left and right,
Bursting surge on the reef, drenching storms on the height.   285
So the folk of Vaiau sailed and were glad all day,
Coasting the palm-tree cape and crossing the populous bay
By all the towns of the Tevas; and still as they bowled
   along,
Boat would answer to boat with jest and laughter and song,
And the people of all the towns trooped to the sides of the
   sea   290
And gazed from under the hand or sprang aloft on the tree,
Hailing and cheering. Time failed them for more to do;
The holiday village careened to the wind, and was gone
   from view
Swift as a passing bird; and ever as onward it bore,
Like the cry of the passing bird, bequeathed its song to the
   shore –   295
Desirable laughter of maids and the cry of delight of the
   child.
And the gazer, left behind, stared at the wake and smiled.
By all the towns of the Tevas they went, and Pápara last,
The home of the chief, the place of muster in war; and
   passed
The march of the lands of the clan, to the lands of an alien
   folk.   300
And there, from the dusk of the shoreside palms, a column
   of smoke
Mounted and wavered and died in the gold of the setting
   sun,
'Paea!' they cried. 'It is Paea.' And so was the voyage done.

In the early fall of the night, Hiopa came to the shore,
And beheld and counted the comers, and lo, they were
   forty score: 305
The pelting feet of the babes that ran already and played,
The clean-lipped smile of the boy, the slender breasts of the
   maid,
And mighty limbs of women, stalwart mothers of men.
The sires stood forth unabashed; but a little back from his
   ken
Clustered the scarcely nubile, the lads and maids, in a ring,   310
Fain of each other, afraid of themselves, aware of the king
And aping behaviour, but clinging together with hands and
   eyes,
With looks that were kind like kisses, and laughter tender
   as sighs.
There, too, the grandsire stood, raising his silver crest,
And the impotent hands of a suckling groped in his barren
   breast.   315
The childhood of love, the pair well married, the innocent
   brood,
The tale of the generations repeated and ever renewed –
Hiopa beheld them together, all the ages of man,
And a moment shook in his purpose.

                  But these were the foes of his clan,   320
And he trod upon pity, and came, and civilly greeted the
   king,
And gravely entreated Rahéro; and for all that could fight
   or sing,
And claimed a name in the land, had fitting phrases of
   praise;
But with all who were well-descended he spoke of the
   ancient days.
And ''Tis true,' said he, 'that in Paea the victual rots on the
   ground;   325
But, friends, your number is many; and pigs must be
   hunted and found,
And the lads troop to the mountains to bring the féis down,
And around the bowls of the kava cluster the maids of the
   town.

So, for tonight, sleep here; but king, common, and priest
Tomorrow, in order due, shall sit with me in the feast.'   330
Sleepless the live-long night, Hiopa's followers toiled.
The pigs screamed and were slaughtered; the spars of the
    guest-house oiled,
The leaves spread on the floor. In many a mountain glen
The moon drew shadows of trees on the naked bodies of
    men
Plucking and bearing fruits; and in all the bounds of the
    town   335
Red glowed the cocoanut fires, and were buried and
    trodden down.
Thus did seven of the yottowas toil with their tale of the
    clan,
But the eighth wrought with his lads, hid from the sight of
    man.
In the deeps of the woods they laboured, piling the fuel high
In faggots, the load of man, fuel seasoned and dry,   340
Thirsty to seize upon fire and apt to blurt into flame.

And now was the day of the feast. The forests, as morning
    came,
Tossed in the wind, and the peaks quaked in the blaze of the
    day
And the cocoanuts showered on the ground, rebounding
    and rolling away:
A glorious morn for a feast, a famous wind for a fire.   345
To the hall of feasting Hiopa led them, mother and sire
And maid and babe in a tale, the whole of the holiday
    throng.
Smiling they came, garlanded green, not dreaming of
    wrong;
And for every three, a pig, tenderly cooked in the ground,
Waited; and féi, the staff of life, heaped in a mound   350
For each where he sat; – for each, bananas roasted and raw
Piled with a bountiful hand, as for horses hay and straw
Are stacked in a stable; and fish, the food of desire,
And plentiful vessels of sauce, and breadfruit gilt in the fire;
And kava was common as water. Feasts have there been
    ere now,   355

And many, but never a feast like that of the folk of Vaiau.
All day long they ate with the resolute greed of brutes,
And turned from the pigs to the fish, and again from the
    fish to the fruits,
And emptied the vessels of sauce, and drank of the kava
    deep;
Till the young lay stupid as stones, and the strongest
    nodded to sleep.   360
Sleep that was mighty as death and blind as a moonless
    night
Tethered them hand and foot; and their souls were
    drowned, and the light
Was cloaked from their eyes. Senseless together, the old and
    the young,
The fighter deadly to smite and the prater cunning of
    tongue,
The woman wedded and fruitful, inured to the pangs of
    birth,   365
And the maid that knew not of kisses, blindly sprawled on
    the earth.
From the hall Hiopa the king and his chiefs came stealthily
    forth.
Already the sun hung low and enlightened the peaks of the
    north;
But the wind was stubborn to die and blew as it blows at
    morn,
Showering the nuts in the dusk, and e'en as a banner is
    torn,   370
High on the peaks of the island, shattered the mountain
    cloud.
And now at once, at a signal, a silent, emulous crowd
Set hands to the work of death, hurrying to and fro,
Like ants, to furnish the faggots, building them broad and
    low,
And piling them high and higher around the walls of the
    hall.   375
Silence persisted within, for sleep lay heavy on all;
But the mother of Támatéa stood at Hiopa's side,
And shook for terror and joy like a girl that is a bride.
Night fell on the toilers, and first Hiopa the wise

Made the round of the house, visiting all with his eyes;   380
And all was piled to the eaves, and fuel blockaded the door;
And within, in the house beleaguered, slumbered the forty
     score.
Then was an aito dispatched and came with fire in his
     hand,
And Hiopa took it. – 'Within,' said he, 'is the life of a land;
And behold! I breathe on the coal, I breathe on the dales of
     the east,   385
And silence falls on forest and shore; the voice of the feast
Is quenched, and the smoke of cooking; the rooftree decays
     and falls
On the empty lodge, and the winds subvert deserted walls.'

Therewithal, to the fuel, he laid the glowing coal;
And the redness ran in the mass and burrowed within like
     a mole,   390
And copious smoke was conceived. But, as when a dam is
     to burst,
The water lips it and crosses in silver trickles at first,
And then, of a sudden, whelms and bears it away
     forthright:
So now, in a moment, the flame sprang and towered in the
     night,
And wrestled and roared in the wind, and high over house
     and tree,   395
Stood, like a streaming torch, enlightening land and sea.

But the mother of Támatéa threw her arms abroad,
'Pyre of my son's,' she shouted, 'debited vengeance of God,
Late, late, I behold you, yet I behold you at last,
And glory, beholding! For now are the days of my agony
     past,   400
The lust that famished my soul now eats and drinks its
     desire,
And they that encompassed my son shrivel alive in the fire.
Tenfold precious the vengeance that comes after lingering
     years!
Ye quenched the voice of my singer? – hark, in your dying
     ears,

The song of the conflagration! Ye left me a widow alone?   405
– Behold, the whole of your race consumes, sinew and bone
And torturing flesh together: man, mother, and maid
Heaped in a common shambles; and already, borne by the
    trade,
The smoke of your dissolution darkens the stars of night.'

Thus she spoke, and her stature grew in the people's sight.   410

3 RAHÉRO

Rahéro was there in the hall asleep: beside him his wife,
Comely, a mirthful woman, one that delighted in life;
And a girl that was ripe for marriage, shy and sly as a
    mouse;
And a boy, a climber of trees: all the hopes of his house.
Unwary, with open hands, he slept in the midst of his folk,   415
And dreamed that he heard a voice crying without, and
    awoke,
Leaping blindly afoot like one from a dream that he fears.
A hellish glow and clouds were about him; – it roared in his
    ears
Like the sound of the cataract fall that plunges sudden and
    steep;
And Rahéro swayed as he stood, and his reason was still
    asleep.   420
Now the flame struck hard on the house, wind-wielded, a
    fracturing blow,
And the end of the roof was burst and fell on the sleepers
    below;
And the lofty hall, and the feast, and the prostrate bodies of
    folk,
Shone red in his eyes a moment, and then were swallowed
    of smoke.
In the mind of Rahéro clearness came; and he opened his
    throat;   425
And as when a squall comes sudden, the straining sail of a
    boat
Thunders aloud and bursts, so thundered the voice of the
    man.

– 'The wind and the rain!' he shouted, the mustering word
   of the clan,
And 'up!' and 'to arms, men of Vaiau!' But silence replied,
Or only the voice of the gusts of the fire, and nothing beside.   430

Rahéro stooped and groped. He handled his womankind,
But the fumes of the fire and the kava had quenched the life
   of their mind,
And they lay like pillars prone; and his hand encountered
   the boy,
And there sprang in the gloom of his soul a sudden
   lightning of joy.
'Him can I save!' he thought, 'if I were speedy enough.'   435
And he loosened the cloth from his loins, and swaddled the
   child in the stuff;
And about the strength of his neck he knotted the burden
   well.

There where the roof had fallen, it roared like the mouth of
   hell.
Thither Rahéro went, stumbling on senseless folk,
And grappled a post of the house, and began to climb in the
   smoke: 440
The last alive of Vaiau; and the son borne by the sire.
The post glowed in the grain with ulcers of eating fire,
And the fire bit to the blood and mangled his hands and
   thighs;
And the fumes sang in his head like wine and stung in his
   eyes;
And still he climbed, and came to the top, the place of proof,   445
And thrust a hand through the flame, and clambered alive
   on the roof.
But even as he did so, the wind, in a garment of flames and
   pain,
Wrapped him from head to heel; and the waistcloth parted
   in twain;
And the living fruit of his loins dropped in the fire below.

About the blazing feast-house clustered the eyes of the foe,   450
Watching, hand upon weapon, lest ever a soul should flee,

Shading the brow from the glare, straining the neck to see.
Only, to leeward, the flames in the wind swept far and wide,
And the forest sputtered on fire; and there might no man
    abide.
Thither Rahéro crept, and dropped from the burning eaves,   455
And crouching low to the ground, in a treble covert of
    leaves
And fire and volleying smoke, ran for the life of his soul
Unseen; and behind him under a furnace of ardent coal,
Cairned with a wonder of flame, and blotting the night with
    smoke,
Blazed and were smelted together the bones of all his folk.   460

He fled unguided at first; but hearing the breakers roar,
Thitherward shaped his way, and came at length to the
    shore.
Sound-limbed he was: dry-eyed; but smarted in every part;
And the mighty cage of his ribs heaved on his straining
    heart
With sorrow and rage. And 'Fools!' he cried, 'fools of Vaiau,   465
Heads of swine – gluttons – Alas! and where are they now?
Those that I played with, those that nursed me, those that I
    nursed?
God, and I outliving them! I, the least and the worst –
I, that thought myself crafty; snared by this herd of swine,
In the tortures of hell and desolate, stripped of all that was
    mine: 470
All! – my friends and my fathers – the silver heads of yore
That trooped to the council, the children that ran to the
    open door
Crying with innocent voices and clasping a father's knees!
And mine, my wife – my daughter – my sturdy climber of
    trees,
Ah, never to climb again!'   475
                    Thus in the dusk of the night
(For clouds rolled in the sky and the moon was swallowed
    from sight),
Pacing and gnawing his fists, Rahéro raged by the shore.
Vengeance: that must be his. But much was to do before;
And first a single life to be snatched from a deadly place,   480

A life, the root of revenge, surviving plant of the race:
And next the race to be raised anew, and the lands of the
    clan
Repeopled. So Rahéro designed, a prudent man
Even in wrath, and turned for the means of revenge and
    escape:
A boat to be seized by stealth, a wife to be taken by rape.   485

Still was the dark lagoon; beyond on the coral wall,
He saw the breakers shine, he heard them bellow and fall.
Alone, on the top of the reef, a man with a flaming brand
Walked, gazing and pausing, a fish-spear poised in his
    hand.
The foam boiled to his calf when the mightier breakers
    came,   490
And the torch shed in the wind scattering tufts of flame.
Afar on the dark lagoon a canoe lay idly at wait:
A figure dimly guiding it: surely the fisherman's mate.
Rahéro saw and he smiled. He straightened his mighty
    thews:
Naked, with never a weapon, and covered with scorch and
    bruise,   495
He straightened his arms, he filled the void of his body with
    breath,
And, strong as the wind in his manhood, doomed the fisher
    to death.
Silent he entered the water, and silently swam, and came
There where the fisher walked, holding on high the flame.
Loud on the pier of the reef volleyed the breach of the sea;   500
And hard at the back of the man, Rahéro crept to his knee
On the coral, and suddenly sprang and seized him, the elder
    hand
Clutching the joint of his throat, the other snatching the
    brand
Ere it had time to fall, and holding it steady and high.
Strong was the fisher, brave, and swift of mind and of eye –   505
Strongly he threw in the clutch; but Rahéro resisted the
    strain,
And jerked, and the spine of life snapped with a crack in
    twain,

And the man came slack in his hands and tumbled a lump
    at his feet.

One moment: and there, on the reef, where the breakers
    whitened and beat,
Rahéro was standing alone, glowing and scorched and
    bare,   510
A victor unknown of any, raising the torch in the air.
But once he drank of his breath, and instantly set him to
    fish
Like a man intent upon supper at home and a savoury dish.
For what should the woman have seen? A man with a
    torch – and then
A moment's blur of the eyes – and a man with a torch
    again.   515
And the torch had scarcely been shaken. 'Ah, surely,'
    Rahéro said,
'She will deem it a trick of the eyes, a fancy born in the
    head;
But time must be given the fool to nourish a fool's belief.'
So for a while, a sedulous fisher, he walked the reef,
Pausing at times and gazing, striking at times with the
    spear: 520
– Lastly, uttered the call; and even as the boat drew near;
Like a man that was done with its use, tossed the torch in
    the sea.

Lightly he leaped on the boat beside the woman; and she
Lightly addressed him, and yielded the paddle and place to
    sit;
For now the torch was extinguished the night was black as
    the pit.   525
Rahéro set him to row, never a word he spoke,
And the boat sang in the water urged by his vigorous
    stroke.
– 'What ails you?' the woman asked, 'and why did you drop
    the brand?'
We have only to kindle another as soon as we come to
    land.'
Never a word Rahéro replied, but urged the canoe.   530

And a chill fell on the woman. – 'Atta! speak! is it you?
Speak! Why are you silent? Why do you bend aside?
Wherefore steer to the seaward?' thus she panted and cried.
Never a word from the oarsman, toiling there in the dark;
But right for a gate of the reef he silently headed the bark,   535
And wielding the single paddle with passionate sweep on
    sweep,
Drove her, the little fitted, forth on the open deep.
And fear, there where she sat, froze the woman to stone:
Not fear of the crazy boat and the weltering deep alone;
But a keener fear of the night, the dark, and the ghostly
    hour,   540
And the thing that drove the canoe with more than a
    mortal's power
And more than a mortal's boldness. For much she knew of
    the dead
That haunt and fish upon reefs, toiling, like men, for bread,
And traffic with human fishers, or slay them and take their
    ware,
Till the hour when the star of the dead goes down, and the
    morning air   545
Blows, and the cocks are singing on shore. And surely she
    knew
The speechless thing at her side belonged to the grave.
                                                   It blew
All night from the south; all night, Rahéro contended and
    kept
The prow to the cresting sea; and, silent as though she
    slept,   550
The woman huddled and quaked. And now was the peep of
    day.
High and long on their left the mountainous island lay;
And over the peaks of Taiárapu arrows of sunlight struck.
On shore the birds were beginning to sing: the ghostly ruck
Of the buried had long ago returned to the covered grave;   555
And here on the sea, the woman, waxing suddenly brave,
Turned her swiftly about and looked in the face of the man.
And sure he was none that she knew, none of her country
    or clan:
A stranger, mother-naked, and marred with the marks of
    fire,   560

But comely and great of stature, a man to obey and admire.
And Rahéro regarded her also, fixed, with a frowning face,
Judging the woman's fitness to mother a warlike race.
Broad of shoulder, ample of girdle, long in the thigh,
Deep of bosom she was, and bravely supported his eye.

'Woman,' said he, 'last night the men of your folk –   565
Man, woman, and maid, smothered my race in smoke.
It was done like cowards; and I, a mighty man of my hands,
Escaped, a single life; and now to the empty lands
And smokeless hearths of my people, sail, with yourself,
    alone.
Before your mother was born, the die of today was thrown   570
And you selected: – your husband, vainly striving, to fall
Broken between these hands: – yourself to be severed from
    all,
The places, the people, you love – home, kindred, and
    clan –
And to dwell in a desert and bear the babes of a kinless
    man.'

Heather Ale

A Galloway Legend

From the bonny bells of heather
    They brewed a drink long-syne,
Was sweeter far than honey,
    Was stronger far than wine.
They brewed it and they drank it,   5
    And lay in a blessed swound
For days and days together
    In their dwellings underground.

There rose a king in Scotland,
    A fell man to his foes,   10

He smote the Picts in battle,
  He hunted them like roes.
Over miles of the red mountain
  He hunted as they fled,
And strewed the dwarfish bodies   15
  Of the dying and the dead.

Summer came in the country,
  Red was the heather bell;
But the manner of the brewing
  Was none alive to tell.   20
In graves that were like children's
  On many a mountain's head,
The Brewsters of the Heather
  Lay numbered with the dead.

The king in the red moorland   25
  Rode on a summer's day;
And the bees hummed, and the curlews
  Cried beside the way.
The king rode, and was angry,
  Black was his brow and pale,   30
To rule in a land of heather
  And lack the Heather Ale.

It fortuned that his vassals,
  Riding free on the heath,
Came on a stone that was fallen   35
  And vermin hid beneath.
Rudely plucked from their hiding,
  Never a word they spoke:
A son and his aged father –
  Last of the dwarfish folk.   40

The king sat high on his charger,
  He looked on the little men;
And the dwarfish and swarthy couple
  Looked at the king again.
Down by the shore he had them: 45
  And there on the giddy brink –

'I will give you life, ye vermin,
    For the secret of the drink.'

There stood the son and father
    And they looked high and low;   50
The heather was red around them,
    The sea rumbled below.
And up and spoke the father,
    Shrill was his voice to hear:
'I have a word in private,   55
    A word for the royal ear.

'Life is dear to the aged,
    And honour a little thing;
I would gladly sell the secret,'
    Quoth the Pict to the King.   60
His voice was small as a sparrow's,
    And shrill and wonderful clear:
'I would gladly sell my secret,
    Only my son I fear.

'For life is a little matter,   65
    And death is nought to the young;
And I dare not sell my honour
    Under the eye of my son.
Take *him*, O king, and bind him,
    And cast him far in the deep;   70
And it's I will tell the secret
    That I have sworn to keep.'

They took the son and bound him,
    Neck and heels in a thong,
And a lad took him and swung him,   75
    And flung him far and strong,
And the sea swallowed his body,
    Like that of a child of ten;
And there on the cliff stood the father,
    Last of the dwarfish men.   80

'True was the word I told you:
　　Only my son I feared;
For I doubt the sapling courage
　　That goes without the beard.
But now in vain is the torture,　　　　　　　　　85
　　Fire shall never avail:
Here dies in my bosom
　　The secret of Heather Ale.'

from **Songs of Travel (1895)**

The Vagabond

To an air of Schubert

Give to me the life I love,
　　Let the lave go by me,
Give the jolly heaven above
　　And the byway nigh me.
Bed in the bush with stars to see,　　　　　　　5
　　Bread I dip in the river –
There's the life for a man like me;
　　There's the life for ever.

Let the blow fall soon or late,
　　Let what will be o'er me;　　　　　　　　　　10
Give the face of earth around
　　And the road before me.
Wealth I seek not, hope nor love,
　　Nor a friend to know me;
All I seek, the heaven above　　　　　　　　　　15
　　And the road below me.

Or let autumn fall on me
   Where afield I linger,
Silencing the bird on tree,
   Biting the blue finger.
White as meal the frosty field –
   Warm the fireside haven –
Not to autumn will I yield,
   Not to winter even!

Let the blow fall soon or late,
   Let what will be o'er me;
Give the face of earth around,
   And the road before me.
Wealth I ask not, hope nor love,
   Nor a friend to know me;
All I ask the heaven above,
   And the road below me.

I will make you brooches . . .

I will make you brooches and toys for your delight
Of bird-song at morning and star-shine at night.
I will make a palace fit for you and me
Of green days in forests and blue days at sea.

I will make my kitchen, and you shall keep your room,
Where white flows the river and bright blows the broom,
And you shall wash your linen and keep your body white
In rainfall at morning and dewfall at night.

And this shall be for music when no one else is near,
The fine song for singing, the rare song to hear!
That only I remember, that only you admire,
Of the broad road that stretches and the roadside fire.

Bright is the ring of words . . .

Bright is the ring of words
　　When the right man rings them,
Fair the fall of songs
　　When the singer sings them.
Still they are carolled and said –   5
　　On wings they are carried –
After the singer is dead
　　And the maker buried.

Low as the singer lies
　　In the field of heather,   10
Songs of his fashion bring
　　The swains together.
And when the west is red
　　With the sunset embers,
The lover lingers and sings   15
　　And the maid remembers.

In the highlands,
in the country places . . .

In the highlands, in the country places,
Where the old plain men have rosy faces,
And the young fair maidens
Quiet eyes;
Where essential silence cheers and blesses,   5
And for ever in the hill-recesses
Her more lovely music
Broods and dies.

O to mount again where erst I haunted;
Where the old red hills are bird-enchanted,   10
And the low green meadows
Bright with sward;
And when even dies, the million-tinted,
And the night has come, and planets glinted,
Lo, the valley hollow   15
Lamp-bestarred!

O to dream, O to awake and wander
There, and with delight to take and render,
Through the trance of silence,
Quiet breath;   20
Lo! for there, among the flowers and grasses,
Only the mightier movement sounds and passes;
Only winds and rivers,
Life and death.

To the Tune of Wandering Willie

Home no more home to me, whither must I wander?
   Hunger my driver, I go where I must.
Cold blows the winter wind over hill and heather;
   Thick drives the rain, and my roof is in the dust.
Loved of wise men was the shade of my roof-tree.   5
   The true word of welcome was spoken in the door –
Dear days of old, with the faces in the firelight,
   Kind folks of old, you come again no more.

Home was home then, my dear, full of kindly faces,
   Home was home then, my dear, happy for the child.   10
Fire and the windows bright glittered on the moorland;
   Song, tuneful song, built a palace in the wild.
Now, when day dawns on the brow of the moorland,
   Lone stands the house, and the chimney-stone is cold.
Lone let it stand, now the friends are all departed,   15
   The kind hearts, the true hearts, that loved the place of old.

Spring shall come, come again, calling up the moorfowl,
   Spring shall bring the sun and rain, bring the bees and flowers;
Red shall the heather bloom over hill and valley,
   Soft flow the stream through the even-flowing hours;   20
Fair the day shine as it shone on my childhood –
   Fair shine the day on the house with open door;
Birds come and cry there and twitter in the chimney –
   But I go for ever and come again no more.

My Wife

     Trusty, dusky, vivid, true,
     With eyes of gold and bramble-dew,
     Steel-true and blade-straight,
     The great artificer
     Made my mate.   5

Honour, anger, valour, fire;
A love that life could never tire,
Death quench or evil stir,
The mighty master
Gave to her.   10

Teacher, tender comrade, wife,
A fellow-farer true through life,
Heart-whole and soul-free
The august father
Gave to me.   15

To an Island Princess

Since long ago, a child at home,
I read and longed to rise and roam,
Where'er I went, whate'er I willed,
One promised land my fancy filled.
Hence the long roads my home I made;   5
Tossed much in ships; have often laid
Below the uncurtained sky my head,
Rain-deluged and wind-buffeted:
And many a thousand hills I crossed
And corners turned – Love's labour lost,   10
Till, Lady, to your isle of sun
I came, not hoping; and, like one
Snatched out of blindness, rubbed my eyes,
And hailed my promised land with cries.

Yes, Lady, here I was at last;   15
Here found I all I had forecast:
The long roll of the sapphire sea
That keeps the land's virginity;
The stalwart giants of the wood
Laden with toys and flowers and food;   20

The precious forest pouring out
To compass the whole town about;
The town itself with streets of lawn,
Loved of the moon, blessed by the dawn,
Where the brown children all the day　　　　25
Keep up a ceaseless noise of play,
Play in the sun, play in the rain,
Nor ever quarrel or complain;
And late at night, in the woods of fruit,
Hark! do you hear the passing flute?　　　　30

I threw one look to either hand,
And knew I was in Fairyland.
And yet one point of being so,
I lacked. For, Lady (as you know),
Whoever by his might of hand,　　　　35
Won entrance into Fairyland,
Found always with admiring eyes
A Fairy princess kind and wise.
It was not long I waited; soon
Upon my threshold, in broad noon,　　　　40
Gracious and helpful, wise and good,
The Fairy Princess Moë stood.

To Kalakaua

With a present of a Pearl

The Silver Ship, my King – that was her name
In the bright islands whence your fathers came –
The Silver Ship, at rest from winds and tides,
Below your palace in your harbour rides:
And the seafarers, sitting safe on shore,　　　　5
Like eager merchants count their treasure o'er.

One gift they find, one strange and lovely thing,
Now doubly precious since it pleased a king.

The right, my liege, is ancient as the lyre
For bards to give to kings what kings admire.   10
'Tis mine to offer for Apollo's sake;
And since the gift is fitting, yours to take.
To golden hands the golden pearl I bring:
The ocean jewel to the island king.

To Princess Kaiulani

Forth from her land to mine she goes,
The island maid, the island rose,
Light of heart and bright of face:
The daughter of a double race.

Her islands here, in Southern sun,   5
Shall mourn their Kaiulani gone,
And I, in her dear banyan shade,
Look vainly for my little maid.

But our Scots islands far away
Shall glitter with unwonted day,   10
And cast for once their tempests by
To smile in Kaiulani's eye.

To My Old Familiars

Do you remember – can we e'er forget? –
How, in the coiled perplexities of youth,
In our wild climate, in our scowling town,
We gloomed and shivered, sorrowed, sobbed and feared?

The belching winter wind, the missile rain,   5
The rare and welcome silence of the snows,
The laggard morn, the haggard day, the night,
The grimy spell of the nocturnal town,
Do you remember? – Ah, could one forget!

As when the fevered sick that all night long   10
Listed the wind intone, and hear at last
The ever-welcome voice of chanticleer
Sing in the bitter hour before the dawn,
With sudden ardour, these desire the day:
So sang in the gloom of youth the bird of hope;   15
So we, exulting, hearkened and desired.
For lo! as in the palace porch of life
We huddled with chimeras, from within –
How sweet to hear! – the music swelled and fell,
And through the breach of the revolving doors   20
What dreams of splendour blinded us and fled!

I have since then contended and rejoiced;
Amid the glories of the house of life
Profoundly entered, and the shrine beheld:
Yet when the lamp from my expiring eyes   25
Shall dwindle and recede, the voice of love
Fall insignificant on my closing ears,
What sound shall come but the old cry of the wind
In our inclement city? what return
But the image of the emptiness of youth,   30
Filled with the sound of footsteps and that voice
Of discontent and rapture and despair?
So, as in darkness, from the magic lamp,
The momentary pictures gleam and fade
And perish, and the night resurges – these   35
Shall I remember, and then all forget.

The tropics vanish . . .

The tropics vanish, and meseems that I,
From Halkerside, from topmost Allermuir,
Or steep Caerketton, dreaming gaze again.
Far set in fields and woods, the town I see
Spring gallant from the shallows of her smoke,   5
Cragged, spired, and turreted, her virgin fort
Beflagged. About, on seaward-drooping hills,
New folds of city glitter. Last, the Forth
Wheels ample waters set with sacred isles,
And populous Fife smokes with a score of towns.   10

There, on the sunny frontage of a hill,
Hard by the house of kings, repose the dead,
My dead, the ready and the strong of word.
Their works, the salt-encrusted, still survive;
The sea bombards their founded towers; the night   15
Thrills pierced with their strong lamps. The artificers,
One after one, here in this grated cell,
Where the rain erases and the rust consumes,
Fell upon lasting silence. Continents
And continental oceans intervene;   20
A sea uncharted, on a lampless isle,
Environs and confines their wandering child
In vain. The voice of generations dead
Summons me, sitting distant, to arise,
My numerous footsteps nimbly to retrace,   25
And, all mutation over, stretch me down
In that devoted city of the dead.

To S. C.

I heard the pulse of the besieging sea
Throb far away all night. I heard the wind
Fly crying and convulse tumultuous palms.
I rose and strolled. The isle was all bright sand,
And flailing fans and shadows of the palm;   5
The heaven all moon and wind and the blind vault;
The keenest planet slain, for Venus slept.
   The king, my neighbour, with his host of wives,
Slept in the precinct of the palisade;
Where single, in the wind, under the moon,   10
Among the slumbering cabins, blazed a fire,
Sole street-lamp and the only sentinel.
   To other lands and nights my fancy turned –
To London first, and chiefly to your house,
The many-pillared and the well-beloved.   15
There yearning fancy lighted; there again
In the upper room I lay, and heard far off
The unsleeping city murmur like a shell;
The muffled tramp of the Museum guard
Once more went by me; I beheld again   20
Lamps vainly brighten the dispeopled street;
Again I longed for the returning morn,
The awaking traffic, the bestirring birds,
The consentaneous trill of tiny song
That weaves round monumental cornices   25
A passing charm of beauty. Most of all,
For your light foot I wearied, and your knock
That was the glad réveillé of my day.
   Lo, now, when to your task in the great house
At morning through the portico you pass,   30
One moment glance, where by the pillared wall
Far-voyaging island gods, begrimmed with smoke,
Sit now unworshipped, the rude monument
Of faiths forgot and races undivined:
Sit now disconsolate, remembering well   35
The priest, the victim, and the songful crowd,
The blaze of the blue noon, and the huge voice,

Incessant, of the breakers on the shore.
As far as these from their ancestral shrine,
So far, so foreign, your divided friends   40
Wander, estranged in body, not in mind.

The Woodman

In all the grove, nor stream nor bird
Nor aught beside my blows was heard,
And the woods wore their noonday dress –
The glory of their silentness.
From the island summit to the seas,   5
Trees mounted, and trees drooped, and trees
Groped upward in the gaps. The green
Inarboured talus and ravine
By fathoms. By the multitude,
The rugged columns of the wood   10
And bunches of the branches stood;
Thick as a mob, deep as a sea,
And silent as eternity.

With lowered axe, with backward head,
Late from this scene my labourer fled,   15
And with a ravelled tale to tell,
Returned. Some denizen of hell,
Dead man or disinvested god,
Had close behind him peered and trod,
And triumphed when he turned to flee.   20
How different fell the lines with me!
Whose eye explored the dim arcade
Impatient of the uncoming shade –
Shy elf, or dryad pale and cold,
Or mystic lingerer from of old: 25
Vainly. The fair and stately things,
Impassive as departed kings,
All still in the wood's stillness stood,

And dumb. The rooted multitude
Nodded and brooded, bloomed and dreamed,   30
Unmeaning, undivined. It seemed
No other art, no hope, they knew,
Than clutch the earth and seek the blue.
Mid vegetable king and priest
And stripling, I (the only beast)   35
Was at the beast's work, killing; hewed
The stubborn roots across, bestrewed
The glebe with the dislustred leaves,
And bade the saplings fall in sheaves;
Bursting across the tangled math   40
A ruin that I called a path,
A Golgotha that, later on,
When rains had watered, and suns shone,
And seeds enriched the place, should bear
And be called garden. Here and there,   45
I spied and plucked by the green hair
A foe more resolute to live,
The toothed and killing sensitive.
He, semi-conscious, fled the attack;
He shrank and tucked his branches back;   50
And straining by his anchor-strand,
Captured and scratched the rooting hand.
I saw him crouch, I felt him bite;
And straight my eyes were touched with sight.
I saw the wood for what it was: 55
The lost and the victorious cause,
The deadly battle pitched in line,
Saw silent weapons cross and shine:
Silent defeat, silent assault,
A battle and a burial vault.   60

Thick round me in the teeming mud
Briar and fern strove to the blood:
The hooked liana in his gin
Noosed his reluctant neighbours in:
There the green murderer throve and spread,   65
Upon his smothering victims fed,
And wantoned on his climbing coil.

Contending roots fought for the soil
Like frightened demons: with despair
Competing branches pushed for air.   70
Green conquerors from overhead
Bestrode the bodies of their dead:
The Caesars of the sylvan field,
Unused to fail, foredoomed to yield:
For in the groins of branches, lo!   75
The cancers of the orchid grow.
Silent as in the listed ring
Two chartered wrestlers strain and cling;
Dumb as by yellow Hooghly's side
The suffocating captives died;   80
So hushed the woodland warfare goes
Unceasing; and the silent foes
Grapple and smother, strain and clasp
Without a cry, without a gasp.
Here also sound thy fans, O God,   85
Here too thy banners move abroad:
Forest and city, sea and shore,
And the whole earth, thy threshing-floor!
The drums of war, the drums of peace,
Roll through our cities without cease,   90
And all the iron halls of life
Ring with the unremitting strife.

The common lot we scarce perceive.
Crowds perish, we nor mark nor grieve:
The bugle calls – we mourn a few!   95
What corporal's guard at Waterloo?
What scanty hundreds more or less
In the man-devouring Wilderness?
What handful bled on Delhi ridge?
– See, rather, London, on thy bridge   100
The pale battalions trample by,
Resolved to slay, resigned to die.
Count, rather, all the maimed and dead
In the unbrotherly war of bread.
See, rather, under sultrier skies   105
What vegetable Londons rise,

And teem, and suffer without sound:
Or in your tranquil garden ground,
Contented, in the falling gloom,
Saunter and see the roses bloom.   110
That these might live, what thousands died!
All day the cruel hoe was plied;
The ambulance barrow rolled all day;
Your wife, the tender, kind, and gay,
Donned her long gauntlets, caught the spud,   115
And bathed in vegetable blood;
And the long massacre now at end,
See! where the lazy coils ascend,
See, where the bonfire sputters red
At even, for the innocent dead.   120

Why prate of peace? when, warriors all,
We clank in harness into hall,
And ever bare upon the board
Lies the necessary sword.
In the green field or quiet street,   125
Besieged we sleep, beleaguered eat;
Labour by day and wake o' nights,
In war with rival appetites.
The rose on roses feeds; the lark
On larks. The sedentary clerk   130
All morning with a diligent pen
Murders the babes of other men;
And like the beasts of wood and park,
Protects his whelps, defends his den.

Unshamed the narrow aim I hold;   135
I feed my sheep, patrol my fold;
Breathe war on wolves and rival flocks,
A pious outlaw on the rocks
Of God and morning; and when time
Shall bow, or rivals break me, climb   140
Where no undubbed civilian dares,
In my war harness, the loud stairs
Of honour; and my conqueror
Hail me a warrior fallen in war.

Tropic Rain

As the single pang of the blow, when the metal is mingled well,
Rings and lives and resounds in all the bounds of the bell,
So the thunder above spoke with a single tongue,
So in the heart of the mountain the sound of it rumbled and
    clung.
Sudden the thunder was drowned – quenched was the levin
    light –   5
And the angle-spirit of rain laughed out loud in the night.
Loud as the maddened river raves in the cloven glen,
Angel of rain! you laughed and leaped on the roofs of men;
And the sleepers sprang in their beds, and joyed and feared as
    you fell.
You struck, and my cabin quailed; the roof of it roared like a
    bell,   10
You spoke, and at once the mountain shouted and shook with
    brooks.
You ceased, and the day returned, rosy, with virgin looks.

And methought that beauty and terror are only one, not two;
And the world has room for love, and death, and thunder, and
    dew;
And all the sinews of hell slumber in summer air;   15
And the face of God is a rock, but the face of the rock is fair.
Beneficent streams of tears flow at the finger of pain;
And out of the cloud that smites, beneficent rivers of rain.

The Last Sight

Once more I saw him. In the lofty room,
Where oft with lights and company his tongue
Was trump to honest laughter, sate attired
A something in his likeness. 'Look!' said one,
Unkindly kind, 'look up, it is your boy!'   5
And the dread changeling gazed on me in vain.

Sing me a song of a lad that is gone . . .

Sing me a song of a lad that is gone,
   Say, could that lad be I?
Merry of soul he sailed on a day
   Over the sea to Skye.

Mull was astern, Rum on the port,   5
   Eigg on the starboard bow;
Glory of youth glowed in his soul;
   Where is that glory now?

Sing me a song of a lad that is gone,
   Say, could that lad be I?   10
Merry of soul he sailed on a day
   Over the sea to Skye.

Give me again all that was there,
   Give me the sun that shone!
Give me the eyes, give me the soul,   15
   Give me the lad that's gone!

Sing me a song of a lad that is gone,
   Say, could that lad be I?
Merry of soul he sailed on a day
   Over the sea to Skye.   20

Billow and breeze, islands and seas,
   Mountains of rain and sun,
All that was good, all that was fair,
   All that was me is gone.

To S. R. Crockett

On receiving a Dedication

Blows the wind today, and the sun and the rain are flying,
    Blows the wind on the moors today and now,
Where about the graves of the martyrs the whaups are crying,
    My heart remembers how!

Grey recumbent tombs of the dead in desert places,   5
    Standing-stones on the vacant wine-red moor,
Hills of sheep, and the howes of the silent vanished races,
    And winds, austere and pure.

Be it granted me to behold you again in dying,
    Hills of home! and to hear again the call;   10
Hear about the graves of the martyrs the peewees crying,
    And hear no more at all.

Poems first published in fiction and later poems published posthumously

Robin and Ben: or, the Pirate and the Apothecary

Come lend me an attentive ear
A startling moral tale to hear,
Of Pirate Rob and Chemist Ben,
And different destinies of men.

Deep in the greenest of the vales   5
That nestle near the coast of Wales,
The heaving main but just in view,
Robin and Ben together grew,
Together worked and played the fool,
Together shunned the Sunday school,   10
And pulled each other's youthful noses
Around the cots, among the roses.

Together but unlike they grew;
Robin was rough, and through and through,
Bold, inconsiderable, and manly,   15
Like some historic Bruce or Stanley.
Ben had a mean and servile soul,
He robbed not, though he often stole.
He sang on Sunday in the choir,
And tamely capped the passing Squire.   20

At length, intolerant of trammels –
Wild as the wild Bithynian camels,
Wild as the wild sea-eagles – Bob
His widowed dam contrives to rob,
And thus with great originality   25

Effectuates his personality.
Thenceforth his terror-haunted flight
He follows through the starry night;
And with the early morning breeze,
Behold him on the azure seas.   30
The master of a trading dandy
Hires Robin for a go of brandy;
And all the happy hills of home
Vanish beyond the fields of foam.

Ben, meanwhile, like a tin reflector,   35
Attended on the worthy rector;
Opened his eyes and held his breath,
And flattered to the point of death;
And was at last, by that good fairy,
Apprenticed to the Apothecary.   40

So, Ben, while Robin chose to roam,
A rising chemist was at home,
Tended his shop with learnèd air,
Watered his drugs and oiled his hair,
And gave advice to the unwary,   45
Like any sleek apothecary.

Meanwhile upon the deep afar
Robin the brave was waging war,
With other tarry desperadoes
About the latitude of Barbadoes.   50
He knew no touch of craven fear;
His voice was thunder in the cheer;
First, from the main-to'-gallan' high,
The skulking merchantman to spy –
The first to bound upon the deck,   55
The last to leave the sinking wreck.
His hand was steel, his word was law,
His mates regarded him with awe.
No pirate in the whole profession
Held a more honourable position.   60

At length, from years of anxious toil,
Bold Robin seeks his native soil;

Wisely arranges his affairs,
And to his native dale repairs.
The Bristol *Swallow* sets him down   65
Beside the well-remembered town.
He sighs, he spits, he marks the scene,
Proudly he treads the village green;
And free from pettiness and rancour,
Takes lodgings at the 'Crown and Anchor'.   70

Strange, when a man so great and good,
Once more in his home-country stood,
Strange that the sordid clowns should show
A dull desire to have him go.
His clinging breeks, his tarry hat,   75
The way he swore, the way he spat,
A certain quality of manner,
Alarming like the pirate's banner –
Somethng that did not seem to suit all –
Something, O call it bluff, not brutal –   80
Something at least, howe'er it's called,
Made Robin generally black-balled.

His soul was wounded; proud and glum,
Alone he sat and swigged his rum,
And took a great distaste to men   85
Till he encountered Chemist Ben.
Bright was the hour and bright the day,
That threw them in eath other's way;
Glad were their mutual salutations,
Long their respective revelations.   90
Before the inn in sultry weather
They talked of this and that together;
Ben told the tale of his indentures,
And Rob narrated his adventures.
Last, as the point of greatest weight,   95
The pair contrasted their estate,
And Robin, like a boastful sailor,
Despised the other for a tailor.

'See,' he remarked, 'with envy, see
A man with such a fist as me!   100

Bearded and ringed, and big, and brown,
I sit and toss the stingo down,
Hear the gold jingle in my bag –
All won beneath the Jolly Flag!'

Ben moralised and shook his head: 105
'You wanderers earn and eat your bread.
The foe is found, beats or is beaten,
And either how, the wage is eaten.
And after all your pully-hauly
Your proceeds look uncommon small-ly.   110
You had done better here to tarry
Apprentice to the Apothecary.
The silent pirates of the shore
Eat and sleep soft, and pocket more
Than any red, robustious ranger   115
Who picks his farthings hot from danger.
You clank your guineas on the board;
Mine are with several bankers stored.
You reckon riches on your digits,
You dash in chase of Sals and Bridgets,   120
You drink and risk delirium tremens,
Your whole estate a common seaman's!
Regard your friend and school companion,
Soon to be wed to Miss Trevanion
(Smooth, honourable, fat and flowery,   125
With Heaven knows how much land in dowry),
Look at me – am I in good case?
Look at my hands, look at my face;
Look at the cloth of my apparel;
Try me and test me, lock and barrel;   130
And own, to give the devil his due,
I have made more of life than you.
Yet I nor sought nor risked a life;
I shudder at an open knife;
The perilous seas I still avoided   135
And stuck to land whate'er betided.
I had no gold, no marble quarry,
I was a poor apothecary,

Yet here I stand, at thirty-eight,
A man of an assured estate.'   140

'Well,' answered Robin – 'well, and how?'

The smiling chemist tapped his brow.
'Rob,' he replied, 'this throbbing brain
Still worked and hankered after gain.
By day and night, to work my will,   145
It pounded like a powder mill;
And marking how the world went round
A theory of theft it found.
Here is the key to right and wrong:
Steal little, but steal all day long;   150
And this invaluable plan
Marks what is called the Honest Man.
When first I served with Doctor Pill,
My hand was ever in the till.
Now that I am myself a master   155
My gains come softer still and faster.
As thus: on Wednesday, a maid
Came to me in the way of trade.
Her mother, an old farmer's wife,
Required a drug to save her life.   160
'At once, my dear, at once,' I said,
Patted the child upon the head,
Bade her be still a loving daughter,
And filled the bottle up with water.'

'Well, and the mother?' Robin cried.   165

'O she!' said Ben, 'I think she died.'

'Battle and blood, death and disease,
Upon the tainted Tropic seas –
The attendant sharks that chew the cud –
The abhorred scuppers spouting blood –   170
The untended dead, the Tropic sun –
The thunder of the murderous gun –
The cut-throat crew – the Captain's curse –

The tempest blustering worse and worse –
These have I known and these can stand,   175
But you, I settle out of hand!'

Out flashed the cutlass, down went Ben
Dead and rotten, there and then.

Translations From Martial:
In Lupum

XI. 18

Beyond the gates, you gave a farm to till:
I have a larger on my window-sill!
A farm, d'ye say? Is this a farm to you? –
Where for all woods I spy one tuft of rue,
And that so rusty, and so small a thing,   5
One shrill cicada hides it with a wing;
Where one cucumber covers all the plain;
And where one serpent rings himself in vain
To enter wholly; and a single snail
Eats all, and exit fasting – to the jail,   10
Here shall I wait in vain till figs be set,
Or till the spring disclose the violet.
Through all my wilds a tameless mouse careers,
And in that narrow boundary appears,
Huge as the stalking lion of Algiers,   15
Huge as the fabled boar of Calydon.
And all my hay is at one swoop impresst.
By one low-flying swallow for her nest.
Strip god Priapus of each attribute
Here finds he scarce a pedestal to foot.   20
The gathered harvest scarcely brims a spoon;
And all my vintage drips in a cocoon.
Generous are you, but I more generous still:
Take back your farm and hand me half a gill!

In Charidemum

XI. 39

You, Charidemus, who my cradle swung
And watched me all the days that I was young –
You, at whose steps the laziest slaves awake
And both the bailiff and the butler quake –
The barber's suds now blacken with my beard   5
And my rough kisses make the maids afeard:
Still, in your eyes, before your judgement seat,
I am the baby that you used to beat.
You must do all things, unreproved; but I
If once to play or to my love I fly,   10
Big with reproach, I see your eyebrows twitch,
And for the accustomed cane your fingers itch.
If something daintily attired I go,
Straight you exclaim: 'Your father did not so!'
And, frowning, count the bottles on the board,   15
As though my cellar were your private hoard.
Enough, at last! I have borne all I can,
And your own mistress hails me for a man.

If I could arise and travel away . . .

If I could arise and travel away
Over the plains of the night and the day,
I should arrive at a land at last
Where all of our sins and sorrows are past
   And we're done with the ten commandments.   5

The name of the land I must not tell;
Green is the grass and cool the well;
Virtue is easy to find and to keep,

And the sinner may lie at his pleasure and sleep
   By the side of the ten commandments.   10

Income and honour, and glory and gold
Grow on the bushes all over the wold;
And if ever a man has a touch of remorse,
He eats of the flower of the golden gorse,
   And to hell with the ten commanments.   15

He goes to church in his Sunday's best;
He eats and drinks with perfect zest;
And whether he lives in heaven or hell
Is more than you or I can tell;
   But he's done with the ten commandments.   20

To the Hesitating Purchaser

From 'Treasure Island'

If sailor tales to sailor tunes,
   Storm and adventure, heat and cold,
If schooners, islands, and maroons
   And Buccaneers and buried Gold,
And all the old romance, retold   5
   Exactly in the ancient way,
Can please, as me they pleased of old,
   The wiser youngsters of today:
So be it, and fall on! If not,
   If studious youth no longer crave,   10
His ancient appetites forgot,
   Kingston, or Ballantyne the brave,
Or Cooper of the wood and wave:
   So be it, also! And may I
And all my pirates share the grave   15
   Where these and their creations lie!

Pirate Ditty

from 'Treasure Island'

Fifteen men on the Dead Man's Chest –
  Yo-ho-ho, and a bottle of rum!
Drink and the devil had done for the rest –
  Yo-ho-ho, and a bottle of rum!

The Song of the Sword of Alan

from 'Kidnapped'

This is the song of the sword of Alan:
The smith made it,
The fire set it;
Now it shines in the hand of Alan Breck.

Their eyes were many and bright,   5
Swift were they to behold,
Many the hand they guided:
The sword was alone.

The dun deer troop over the hill,
They are many, the hill is one: 10
The dun deer vanish,
The hill remains.

Come to me from the hills of heather,
Come from the isles of the sea.
O far-beholding eagles,   15
Here is your meat.

To Katharine de Mattos

With a copy of 'Dr Jekyll and Mr Hyde'

Bells upon the city are ringing in the night;
High above the gardens are the houses full of light;
On the heathy Pentlands is the curfew flying free,
And the broom is blowing bonnie in the north countrie.

It's ill to break the bonds that God decreed to bind,   5
Still we'll be the children of the heather and the wind.
Far away from home, O, it's still for you and me
That the broom is blowing bonnie in the north countrie!

To My Wife

Found in the Manuscript of 'Weir of Hermiston'

I saw rain falling and the rainbow drawn
On Lammermuir. Hearkening I heard again
In my precipitous city beaten bells
Winnow the keen sea wind. And here afar,
Intent on my own race and place, I wrote.   5
    Take thou the writing: thine it is. For who
Burnished the sword, blew on the drowsy coal,
Held still the target higher, chary of praise
And prodigal of censure – who but thou?
So now, in the end, if this the least be good,   10
If any deed be done, if any fire
Burn in the imperfect page, the praise be thine.

On an Inland Voyage

Who would think, herein to look,
That from these exiguous bounds,
I have dug a printed book
And a cheque for twenty pounds?

Thus do those who trust the Lord   5
Go rejoicing on their way
And receive a great reward
For having been so kind as lay.

Had the fun of the voyage
Had the sport of the boats   10
Who could have hoped in addition
The pleasure of fing'ring the notes?

Yes, sir, I wrote the book; I own the fact
It was, perhaps, sir, an unworthy act.
Have you perused it, sir? – You have? – indeed   15
Then between you and me there no debate is.
I did a silly act, but I was fee'd;
You did a sillier, and you did it gratis!

On Some Ghostly
Companions at A Spa

That was an evil day when I
To Strathpeffer drew anigh,
For there I found no human soul
But Ogres occupied the whole.

They had at first a human air   5
In coats and flannel underwear.
They rose and walked upon their feet

And filled their bellies full of meat.
They wiped their lips when they had done,
But they were Ogres every one.   10

Each issuing from his secret bower,
I marked them in the morning hour.
By limp and totter, lisp and droop,
I singled each one from the group.
I knew them all as they went by –   15
I knew them by their blasted eye!

Detested Ogres, from my sight
Depart to your congenial night!
From these fair vales, from this fair day,
Fleet, spectres, on your downward way,   20
Like changing figures in a dream,
To Muttonhold or Pittenweem!
As, by some harmony divine
The devils quartered in the swine,
If any baser place exist   25
In God's great registration list –
Some den with wallow and a trough –
Find it, ye ogres, and be off!

Brasheanna

Sonnets on Peter Brash, a publican, dedicated to Charles Baxter

3

There let us often wend our pensive way,
    There often pausing celebrate the past;   30
    For though indeed our BRASH be dead at last,
Perchance his spirit, in some minor way,
Nor pure immortal nor entirely dead,
    Contrives upon the farther shore of death
    To pick a rank subsistence, and for breath   35
Breathes ague, and drinks creosote of lead,
There, on the way to that infernal den,

Where burst the flames forth thickly, and the sky
  Flares horrid through the murk methinks he doles
    Damned liquors out to Hellward-faring souls,   40
And as his impotent anger ranges high
Gibbers and gurgles at the shades of men.

Notes and glossary

Duddingston: Duddingston Loch was a favourite skating venue in nineteenth-century Edinburgh.

The Light-Keeper: One of several poems which draws on RLS's lighthouse engineering heritage.

To the Commissioners of the Northern Lights: While still an engineering student, RLS wrote a paper 'On a new form of intermittent light for lighthouses' which he read to the Royal Scottish Society of Arts in March 1871.

To Charles Baxter: Baxter was a fellow law student and one of RLS's closest friends. RLS studied for the Bar when he gave up engineering.
  Iyart – multi-coloured; Dean – the Dean village, on the Water of Leith; Embro – Edinburgh; smoored – smothered, choked; snell – bitter; scowtherin' – withering; Brunteelan' – Burntisland, Fife; sweir – unwilling; blaudin' – pouring, buffeting; bicker – move rapidly, tap; lunted – blazed; sicker – sure, safe.

Underwoods: Although published after *A Child's Garden of Verses* this collection contains many poems written earlier.

A Song of the Road
  gauger – exciseman.

To Will H. Low: RLS met Low (1853–1932), an American painter, in France in 1875.

To Andrew Lang: RLS met Lang (1844–1912), a Scottish poet and folklorist, in 1874.

To W. E. Henley: RLS met Henley (1849–1903), poet and journalist, at Edinburgh's Royal Infirmary where he was being treated for tubercular arthritis. They became close friends and collaborated in the writing of several plays.

Henry James: RLS met James (1843–1916) in Bournemouth in 1885. A warm literary and personal friendship ensued.

The Mirror Speaks: Also a tribute to RLS's friendship with James.
Skerryvore – the name given by RLS to the house in Bournemouth, after the Stevenson-designed Hebridean lighthouse of the same name. See **Skerryvore** and **Skerryvore: the Parallel.**

Requiem: The first draft was written in California in 1880, when RLS was very ill, 14 years before his death in 1894.

In Memoriam F.A.S.:   Bertie Sitwell, the 18-year-old son of Mrs Fanny Sitwell, died of tuberculosis in Davos, Switzerland when RLS was spending the winter there.

A Portrait: A satirical portrait of a W. H. Mallock, a minor literary figure of the period.

A Camp: First published in *Travels with a Donkey* (1879).

The Country of the Camisards: Also dates from RLS's walking trip in the Cevennes in 1878.

Skerryvore: See **The Mirror Speaks.**

Say not of me . . .:   Refers to RLS's pursuit of a literary career rather than engineering like his father and grandfather.

The Maker to Posterity
ripin' – searching; lear – knowledge; spier – ask; mou – mouth; steik – shut; Lallan – Lowland, i.e. Lallans or Lowland Scots; Tantallon – Tantallon Castle on the Berwickshire coast.

Ille Terrarum: The subject of this poem is Swanston Cottage, the Stevenson family country home in the Pentland Hills outside Edinburgh.
nirly – pinching; theek – thatch; auld-farrant – old-fashioned; couthy – comfortable; bien – cosy; pickle – a few; beeks – warms, shines; buss –

bush, thicket; cangle – dispute; orra – uncommon, odd; kittle – skilful, cunning; neukit – cornered; gangrel – tramping; goavin' – wandering; soopit – swept; glaur – mud; hizzie – hussy; tautit – untidy; wean – child; drucken – drunken; blads – blows, buffets; dowie – dull, dismal; cauldrife – cold; kintry – country; bield – shelter; limmer – rogue.

A Lowden Sabbath Morn

lintie – linnet; lave – rest, remainder; raxt – stretched; steerin' – bustling; stoury – dusty; cleiks – links arms with; sonsie – cheery, attractive; yett – gate; gash – respectable; blate – timid, modest; hirplin' – limping; clavers – gossip; prezenter – precentor, leader of the singing in a presbyterian church; hoastin' – coughing; fisslin' – scuffling; preen – pin; waukrif – wakeful.

The Song of Rahéro: RLS heard this legend from Princess Moe of Tautira, Tahiti, when he was the guest of her and her brother Ori a Ori in 1888.

Songs of Travel: First published in 1895 as vol XIV of the Edinburgh Edition of RLS's works, a project under way before his death. It was published separately in 1896 by Chatto and Windus.

To the Tune of Wandering Willie: A traditional Scottish tune to which Burns also wrote words.

My Wife: RLS married Fanny Osbourne, a divorced American with two children, in California in 1880.

To an Island Princess: Princess Moë of Tautira. See **The Song of Rahéro.**

To Kalakaua: King of the Hawaiian Islands, whom RLS got to know in Honolulu in 1889.

To Princess Kaiulani: The daughter of Kalakaua's sister and a Scot, Alexander Cleghorn. She was sent to Scotland to be educated.

To My Old Familiars: RLS's old friends in Edinburgh.

To S.C.: Sidney Colvin (1845–1927) was friend and mentor to RLS for most of his career. He acted as RLS's agent in London when he was in the South Pacific.

The Woodman: Arises from RLS's labours to tame the jungle at Vailima.

The Last Sight: Refers to RLS's father.

Sing me a song of a lad that is gone . . .: Written to a version of a traditional tune added to by Lady Wilson.

To S. R. Crockett: The novelist S. R. Crockett (1860–1914) dedicated *The Stickit Minister* to RLS.

Robin and Ben: or, The Pirate and the Apothecary: First published in *Moral Tales* (1898) with original woodcuts by RLS.

Translations from Martial: RLS read and enjoyed Latin verse although he professed himself not a good Latin scholar.

To the Hesitating Purchaser and **Pirate Ditty:** First published in *Treasure Island* (1893).

The Song of the Sword of Alan: First published in *Kidnapped* (1885).

To Katharine de Mattos: A cousin of RLS.

On Some Ghostly Companions: Refers to RLS's stay at Strathpeffer in Sutherland in August 1880.

Brasheanna: Peter Brash was a notoriously ill-tempered Edinburgh publican.